Misrepresented People

Poetic Responses to Trump's America

Grab them by the pussy.
                    —Donald Trump

Whoever degrades another degrades me,
And whatever is done or said returns at last to me.

Through me the afflatus surging and surging, through me the current
                    and index.

I speak the pass-word primeval, I give the sign of democracy,
By God! I will accept nothing which all cannot have their counterpart
                    of on the same terms.
                    —Walt Whitman

This country has been hostile to its people for a long time. For some
                    of you it is new. For some of you it is not so new.
                    —Tamika Mallory (21 January 2017)

In the so-called "Land of God"
My kind were treated hard.
From back then until now
I see, and you agree—
We have been a misrepresented people.
                    —Stevie Wonder

JOE WEIL

JAMEKA WILLIAMS

PHILLIP B. WILLIAMS

JANE WONG

JAVIER ZAMORA

Introduction

Donald Trump, as a political figure, is perhaps the most perfect expression of American empire: a contradictory amalgam of naïveté and cunning, fueled by unchecked ego, greed, and the desire for unlimited power, gaudy, brash, petulant, cocky, unrepentant, narcissistic, delusional, and foolishly, unjustifiably, confident; his election stands as the most tangible proof of the ignorance, fear, cruelty, violence, apathy, and casual disregard that underwrite daily life in the United States of America. This anthology began in the days after November 8, 2016 as a direct response to Trump's campaign and election. From its inception, this anthology has been a time-bound project with immediate goals: 1) to provide a space for expressions of political dissent and social consciousness, 2) to provide a space for poets from misrepresented and underrepresented groups, 3) to decry the ascendancy of right-wing and reactionary ideologies, 4) to raise money for a worthy charity (The National Immigration Law Center). The book you hold in your hands also celebrates the dynamic pluralism of contemporary poetry. This volume contains work from a variety of aesthetic stances, from poets whose personal backgrounds reflect the vibrant multiplicity of our democratic vistas at their most resplendent. The poets anthologized herein bear witness to, rage against, and defy the misogyny, racism, homophobia, xenophobia, and authoritarian impulses that have always surrounded us, but that are incarnated in the 45th president.

Some of the poems in this anthology chronicle, albeit partially and imperfectly, the unprecedented rise to power of Donald Trump. Many of the poems included in these pages were written either during the campaign or during the first one hundred days of the Trump presidency. Some of the poems were written years before Trump was a viable presidential candidate. All of the poems, both directly and indirectly, address the persistent underlying issues of inequity and injustice that have led to the current political moment; the poems contained in these pages resonate with the vision Martín Espada so eloquently expresses in his poem "How We Could Have Lived or Died This Way":

I see the rebels marching, hands upraised before the riot
  squads,
faces in bandannas against the tear gas, and I walk beside
  them unseen.
I see the poets, who will write the songs of insurrection
  generations unborn
will read or hear a century from now, words that make
  them wonder
how we could have lived or died this way, how the
  descendants of slaves
still fled and the descendants of slave-catchers still shot
  them, how we awoke
every morning without the blood of the dead sweating from
  every pore.

We hope that this anthology will join a chorus of other anthologies aimed at resisting tyranny, bigotry, and provincialism in all of its forms. Although we aimed at inclusiveness in this volume, we recognize that there are many groups who are not represented in these pages. We hope that groups who do not find themselves represented in these pages will continue the work initiated in anthologies like this one. At a time when large swaths of the nation, and of the world, have succumbed to a reality television ontology, the poems collected in this volume offer the terra firma of imaginative empathy only available to us through poetry. We believe in the hard-fought duende of a good poem. We believe that beauty matters. We believe that truth matters. We believe that words matter—on the page, in the digital ether, and in the air. We believe that the voices of poets might counter alternative facts and fake news with the earned communion and the restorative utterance of the lyric and of the narrative. We extend our camaraderie to those of you who believe the same. We extend our love even to those who might oppose us. We echo Whitman by affirming openness as the watchword of true art: "Unscrew the locks from the doors! / Unscrew the doors themselves from their jambs!"

—María Isabel Alvarez & Dante Di Stefano

N.B. We would particularly like to thank Kazim Ali, David Baker, Tom Bouman, Martín Espada, Brian Fanelli, Timothy Green, Martha Rhodes, Nicole Santalucia, Tylonn Sawyer, Christian Teresi, and Leah Umansky for their support of this project. We would like to recognize *Love's Executive Order,* Four Way Books, *Rattle, Rise Up Review,* and *Poetry* for publishing work that inspired this anthology. This volume also owes a debt to Michael Boughn and Kent Johnson's anthology *Resist Much / Obey Little: Inaugural Poems to the Resistance.* Thank you, as well, to our publisher, Raymond Hammond, who had the vision and the heart to champion this anthology and everything it stands for. Thank you, most of all, to our contributors, whose work leaves us breathless and hopeful.

Dedicated to the Memory of Claribel Alegría, Amiri Baraka, Gwendolyn Brooks, Carlos Bulosan, Etheridge Knight, Philip Levine, Audre Lorde, Adrienne Rich, Muriel Rukeyser, & Phillis Wheatley

& for all of those poets whose work has gone unrecognized or is lost and unheard

Hanif Abdurraqib

It's Just That I'm Not Really Into Politics

violence begets more / violence / or so I've been told / but all of
this country's skyscrapers / are still standing / despite the blood
/ that builds a boat underneath the tongue / after speaking its
name / violence begets / more photo opportunities / at the feet
of a burning / temple / I show up to the resistance / and someone
hands me a rose / the color of surrender / violence begets thirst
/ a new thing in need / of clean water / once / towards the black
/ and spotted sky / I raised a fist / inside of a glove / sewn in a
country / torn apart by our bombs / I purchased the gloves in a
store / after midnight / from a cashier who wore a picture / of her
daughter on her chest / and looked as though she might have been
crying / before I arrived / violence begets a hunger for warmth /
at all costs / I sit in a running car / and count all of the things /
yet to be swallowed / by the horned ghosts of empire / If you make
your own prison / you can find your own map / to freedom / the
smoke from all our engines / is beckoning the sun / close / the
oceans are rising / to the height of a child / sitting on a mother's
shoulders / pointing to the horizon with a single / trembling /
finger

& who, this time

will starve the mouths of cocked and eager guns. & who, this time, will
place themselves in front of the machinery of burial. & who, this time,
will kiss under the aching moonlight like the world isn't crumbling
at their backs. & who, this time, will take the babies to the rising river
and let what will be their undoing wash over their heads. & who, this
time, will not run from the fire whispering its way along a city's spine.
& who, this time, will instead break the tree's lowest branch & bend it
into the fire. & who, this time, will carry the torch to the temple gates
& interrupt the crowning & the victory feasts & the death parades
crawling long into the streets. & who, this time, will weigh the price of
heaven in their palms & instead turn to the faces of their people & say
hell is upon us again but this time the hell will be ours and ours alone.
& who, this time, will be the righteous demon & raise up all other
righteous demons to cast out the vicious. & who, this time, will serve
the reminder that there are more of us than there are of them. & who,
this time, will mean that we all have ancestors & some of them built
this country. & some of them were fed into the hunger of war to keep
this country built. & some of them were dragged across Kelly Ingram
Park by the jaws of police dogs. & some of them were pushed like dying
weeds down Birmingham by the riot hoses. & some of them washed
blood out of their only good pair of marching shoes. & some of them
washed blood out of their grandmother's only pair of good sheets.
& some of them buried their children at dawn & pressed their backs
against police barricades at dusk. & some of them fill prisons & hum
the words from a spiritual passed down from their mothers who sit in
empty houses with wide yards, paid for with the money their children
got from doing what a judge said won't have them home for another
twenty. & some of them left behind enough of themselves to rattle us,
coughing, to whatever freedom waits beyond the new & slick walls. &
some of them hover in the night & lock arms above our gathering. &
some of them lean into our ears and share the same small blessing:

they can't kill us
until they kill us.
they can't kill us
until they kill us.
they can't kill us
until they kill us.

they can't kill us.

I Don't Know Any Longer Why the Flags Are at Half-Staff

I think I am breaking up with memory. again. I live
by only that which will still allow me

to do the living. The flag, for example, reminds me
to either feel fear or sadness, depending on how high

it is drawn along its metal spine. I guess I am not breaking up
with all memories: at the summer camp before 7th grade,

my homie Trey stole some rich boy's sonic the hedgehog
underwear and ran them up the flagpole. They were covered in gold

rings. I woke up, and that was my country. I salute whatever cloth I must
in order to keep breathing. I hum every anthem through clenched

teeth. I am, still, a victim of familiar melody. Particularly when it is sung
right, by someone who comes from a long line of people who had to sing

for their meals. Here we are, mouths open in summer. The grief passes
through us without ceremony these days. effortless heartbreak.

I wonder, for a moment, if the land shook hard and rattled the flag
halfway down way back when it felt the arrival

of the first bullet / the first bomb / the first family
torn apart by the fangs of our endless war / the first mother crying

the dead's name into her palms. I'm saying the flag has maybe
always been this way, and I've just recently become bored with

the optimism of pretending. In the hood, the dope boys come back
from a funeral and pour a 40oz of OE out at the center of the basketball court

until the bottle is half-full. Until the bottle is half-empty. Until the bottle
is half what it was before the news of death, and half ready to be consumed.

This, too, is how I walk. Half-empty. Half-full. Half-hearted. Fly,
but with a glance over my shoulder as I turn every block.

In the hood, there aren't enough flags to know when the mourning
is supposed to be over. Or if the flag cuts through the wind and sings

back the name of your homie who got buried and didn't make the news.
From my father's window, a row of boys march the block, one hand

holding up their beltless denim. Saggin' spelled backwards is niggas,
the white cop reminded us past curfew one night back in '01.

Niggas. As in, some of my niggas wear their pants halfway
down their stiff legs. In memory of, in memory of, in memory.

KAVEH AKBAR

Unburnable the Cold is Flooding Our Lives

the prophets are alive but unrecognizable to us
as calligraphy to a mouse   for a time they dragged

long oar strokes across the sky   now they sit
in graveyards drinking coffee forking soapy cottage cheese

into their mouths   my hungry is different than their hungry
I envy their discipline but not enough to do anything about it

I blame my culture   I blame everyone but myself
intent arrives like a call to prayer and is as easy to dismiss

Rumi said the two most important things in life were beauty
and bewilderment   this is likely a mistranslation

after thirty years in America my father now dreams in English
says he misses the dead relatives he used to be able to visit in sleep

how many times are you allowed to lose the same beloveds
before you stop believing they're gone

some migrant birds build their nests over rivers
to push them into the water when they leave   this seems

almost warm   a good harm   the addictions
that were killing me fastest were the ones I loved best

turning the chisel toward myself I found my body
was still the size of my body   still unarmored as wet bread

one way to live a life is to spend each moment asking
forgiveness for the last   it seems to me the significance

of remorse would deflate with each performance   better
to sink a little into the earth and quietly watch life unfold

violent as a bullring   the carpenter's house will always be
the last to be built   sometimes a mind is ready to leave

the world before its body   sometimes paradise happens
too early and leaves us shuddering in its wake

I am glad I still exist   glad for cats and moss
and Turkish indigo   and yet   to be light upon the earth

to be steel bent around an endless black   to once again
be God's own tuning fork   and yet   and yet

Despite My Efforts Even My Prayers Have Turned into Threats

Holy father I can't pretend
I'm not afraid to see you again
but I'll say that when the time
comes I believe my courage
will expand like a sponge
cowboy in water. My earth-
father was far braver than me—
coming to America he knew
no English save Rolling Stones
lyrics and how to say *thanks
God*. Will his goodness roll
over to my tab and if yes, how
soon? I'm sorry for neglecting
your myriad signs, which seem
obvious now as a hawk's head
on an empty plate. I keep waking
up at the bottom of swimming
pools, the water reflecting
whatever I miss most: whiskey-
glass, pill bottles, my mother's
oleander, which was sweet
and evergreen but toxic in all
its parts. I know it was silly
to keep what I kept from you;
you've always been so charmed
by my weaknesses. I just figured
you were becoming fed up with
all your making, like a virtuoso
trying not to smash apart her
flute onstage. Plus, my sins
were practically devotional:
two peaches stolen from
a bodega, which were so sweet
I savored even the bits I flossed
out my teeth. I know it's
no excuse, but even thinking
about them now I'm drooling.
Consider the night I spent reading
another man's lover the *Dream*

Songs in bed—we made it to
"a green living / drops
limply" before we were
tangled into each other, cat
still sleeping at our feet. Allow
me these treasures, Lord.
Time will break what doesn't
bend—even time. Even you.

María Isabel Alvarez

In America

They ask me
What's it like being a brown woman in America?
I want to say
It's like screaming in a dream
And expecting a reaction.

They ask me
What's it like being an immigrant in America?
I want to say
It's like wearing perfume
And everyone is allergic.

They ask me
What's it like praying for change in America?
I want to say
It's like pressing your ear to the dirt
and hoping to hear the sea.

ELOISA AMEZCUA

When Mexico Sends Its People, They're Not Sending Their Best

my father is not rapist
or a drug trafficker or a criminal or a killer or a rapist
or a drug trafficker or a criminal or a killer or a rapist
or a drug trafficker or a criminal or a killer or a rapist
or a drug trafficker or a criminal or a killer or a rapist
or a drug trafficker or a criminal or a killer or a rapist
or a drug trafficker or a criminal or a killer or a rapist
or a drug trafficker or a criminal or a killer or a rapist
or a drug trafficker or a criminal or a killer or a rapist
or a drug trafficker or a criminal or a killer or a rapist
or a drug trafficker or a criminal or a killer or a rapist
or a drug trafficker or a criminal or a killer or a rapist
or a drug trafficker or a criminal or a killer or a rapist
or a bad one

/

my mother is not a rapist
or a drug trafficker or a criminal or a killer or a rapist
or a drug trafficker or a criminal or a killer or a rapist
or a drug trafficker or a criminal or a killer or a rapist
or a drug trafficker or a criminal or a killer or a rapist
or a drug trafficker or a criminal or a killer or a rapist
or a drug trafficker or a criminal or a killer or a rapist
or a drug trafficker or a criminal or a killer or a rapist
or a drug trafficker or a criminal or a killer or a rapist
or a drug trafficker or a criminal or a killer or a rapist
or a drug trafficker or a criminal or a killer or a rapist
or a drug trafficker or a criminal or a killer or a rapist
or a drug trafficker or a criminal or a killer or a rapist
or a bad one

/

I am not a rapist
or a drug trafficker or a criminal or a killer or a rapist
or a drug trafficker or a criminal or a killer or a rapist
or a drug trafficker or a criminal or a killer or a rapist
or a drug trafficker or a criminal or a killer or a rapist
or a drug trafficker or a criminal or a killer or a rapist
or a drug trafficker or a criminal or a killer or a rapist
or a drug trafficker or a criminal or a killer or a rapist
or a drug trafficker or a criminal or a killer or a rapist
or a drug trafficker or a criminal or a killer or a rapist
or a drug trafficker or a criminal or a killer or a rapist
or a drug trafficker or a criminal or a killer or a rapist
or a drug trafficker or a criminal or a killer or a rapist
or a bad one either

/

when America elects a president, they are not electing their best
when America elects a president, they are not electing their best
when America elects a president, they are not electing their best
when America elects a president, they are not electing their best
when America elects a president, they are not electing their best
when America elects a president, they are not electing their best
when America elects a president, they are not electing their best
when America elects a president, they are not electing their best
when America elects a president, they are not electing their best
when America elects a president, they are not electing their best
when America elects a president, they are not electing their best
when America elects a president, they are not electing their best
when America elects a president, they are not electing their best
though they've not yet begun to hear me scream

Elegy

Nov. 9, 2016

I woke up wanting
to have children

less than I wanted
them when I went

to bed. I can't
imagine why I'd

be so careless.
On the news,

a woman
covers her face

with her dark
hands & I stare

at the remains
of her kin covered

with a shiny tarp—
tearless. I look out

the window & see
my neighbor drive past

in her car laughing
perhaps at the radio,

her pale hand reaching
for the dial & for

a moment, I'm
envious of the way

the light turns
her blonde hair

translucent, how
in the backseat

her baby sleeps
unscathed in his

expensive car seat.
I want to laugh

till my womb
falls out

between my legs—
a bloody Rorschach

splatter—& there
is no more wanting.

I know now
how this world

can turn a body
into an urn.

Why I Am Not an Orgasm
after Frank O'Hara

I am not an orgasm. I'm a poet.
Why? I think I'd rather be
an orgasm. But I'm not. Well,

not today. My husband is in
bed, reading the Times.
When I bend to kiss him, he
says, "Lie down, why don't you?"
And I do. The orgasm does, too,
or at least, thinks about it. Together
we slide beneath the sheets.
"You're still reading the news," I sigh.
"Yes," he says. And absently
pats my arm. "What's happening?"
"Donald Trump," he begins.

That's when the orgasm leaves.
It doesn't care for Donald Trump.
Neither do I. I feel so lonesome
then. So bereft. I walk to my
desk and begin to write lists of
random words. Then lines. They
undulate in slow, loopy waves.
They do not tell the truth.

They say that I live in Costa del
Sol, a luminous city of lust and
sand. I am the sexiest woman
alive. The last real blond. Today,
wearing a peach-colored gossamer
gown, I stretch out beneath the
ylang-ylang trees to warm my
nut-brown thighs, and wait for
my beloved to drop in. Hours

go by. The phone rings. The
woman in my poem lights up
a Virginia Slims. *Fuck it,* she
swears, and reaches for her cell.
It's my husband calling to talk
about the latest Breaking News.
I stop writing and stare at the
cigarette butts spilling out
of the crystal ashtray. Outside,
the world races by. My mind
turns to dust and crows. I sip weak
coffee and give the dog a biscuit.
I call the poem, "Orgasm," even if
there's not a single orgasm left
in that fucking seaside town.

William Archila

This is for Henry

It always starts here,
over the chain-linked fence
        with crooked fingers,

leather shoes, running
across the railroad tracks,

        no sound but a gasp
for breath, our white shirts flapping
like flags, cops in black behind.

Sometimes, it's you kneeling
at the corner of the liquor store, handcuffed,
        baton blow
to your back, flopping
to the ground, a grunt
        of flesh and bone,
your golden tooth shining.

This is what I remember
when I drive through east L.A., the boys leaning
        against the wall, rising above trash
            cans, beer bottles,

baggy pants and black
shades, long white shirts
        with two clown faces
above the left breast: one laughing,
            the other crying.

        I think
we were fifteen
when we worked in the dark kitchen,
            restaurant heat
                of vegetables and spices,
bags of rice, boxed beer from China.

During breaks, you stood in the alley,
        your shirt over the shoulder
like a towel, whistling
at the girls strolling

their short skirts, exposing
        the lighter skin
                of their bodies.

Around midnight, after carrying
        the last crate of dishes, we untied
our wet aprons.

                I sat across from you
munching on bread, Italian sausages,
swigging on a bottle of wine,
your talk thick as honey—
                marijuana visions of North
                        America: blonde girls and their bikinis,
                        low riders at night, you in a zoot suit
                                and Bruce Lee.

Fifteen years will pass
before I think of you again,
deportation to a village
        between cane fields at dusk,

        your disappearance between the Eucharist
        and the clang of the bell
                early Sunday morning.

I'm a teacher now,
fingers of chalk, papers piled around me.
        Sometimes, in the dark eyes
        of students, you appear,
                your white shirt, shiny shoes,

                your back slouched
                at the board, cracking the English grammar.

On the street corner, a boy
flashes a hand sign

and it all starts again,
climbing over the fence, running through east L.A.

The Line

I watch them climb the wall,
stumble over tarnished coils
under hills scorched in dry heat
shriveled up like stone. I remember
I jumped a barbed wire fence—
ropes of bristling spikes nailed
against the bark of a tree—
and found a small wooden cross
tilting on the highway shoulder.
I know the body was not shipped
back to the family, given a funeral,
news never reached the father
before he wandered the border towns
seeking his son, his wife
covering her face with an apron.
The small screen flickers, displays
twenty men shackled, single-file
boarding a bus at daylight.
I often wonder about the father
too exhausted to sleep, scuffing
for miles, his journey erratic
as if he does not want to arrive,
the earth below his feet raspy
like ashes. The line stretches
on the page, forges a road
across countries, the entire
length of the coast, always
pulling me to the hour I crossed
the border like a full moon
that rises over rooftops,
my back wet, the blades of the chopper
blasting wind & falling rain.

FATIMAH ASGHAR

If They Should Come for Us

these are my people & I find
them on the street & shadow
through any wild all wild
my people my people
a dance of strangers in my blood
the old woman's sari dissolving to wind
bindi a new moon on her forehead
I claim her my kin & sew
the star of her to my breast
the toddler dangling from stroller
hair a fountain of dandelion seed
at the bakery I claim them too
the sikh uncle at the airport
who apologizes for the pat
down the muslim man who abandons
his car at the traffic light drops
to his knees at the call of the azan
& the muslim man who sips
good whiskey at the start of maghrib
the lone khala at the park
pairing her kurta with crocs
my people my people I can't be lost
when I see you my compass
is brown & gold & blood
my compass a muslim teenager
snapback & high-tops gracing
the subway platform
mashallah I claim them all
my country is made
in my people's image
if they come for you they
come for me too in the dead
of winter a flock of
aunties step out on the sand
their dupattas turn to ocean

a colony of uncles grind their palms
& a thousand jasmines bell the air
my people I follow you like constellations
we hear the glass smashing the street
& the nights opening their dark
our names this country's wood
for the fire my people my people
the long years we've survived the long
years yet to come I see you map
my sky the light your lantern long
ahead & I follow I follow

CHAUN BALLARD

Pantoum on the Presidential Election (from Saudi Arabia)

Fall is tolerable here in Jeddah.
Still, I keep the AC on. My middle-high
students are keeping me up-to-date
on the presidential election.

Still, I keep the AC on. The middle-high
faithfully follow the news, I mean down
to the minute. *What do you think about the presidential
election?* they ask. *Who do you want to win?*

Faithfully following the news, my students
believe Hillary can't be trusted. *Trump
is crazy,* they say. *Who do you want to win?*
Abdulrahman retells a joke,

believes Hillary can't be trusted, and Trump
hates Muslims and Mexicans.
Abdulrahman retells a joke:
If Hillary and Trump are in a boat—

Hates Muslims and Mexicans, I think to myself.
The teacher in me wants to respond: *Hate is such a strong word.*
But I allow him to continue. *If Hillary and Trump are in a boat
and it capsizes, who survives?*

The teacher in me wants to respond: *Hate is such a strong word.*
My wife sends me a message, says colleagues are offering condolences.
Abdulrahman presses: *If it capsizes, Mr. Chaun, who survives?*
I want to say I don't understand the question.

Why are people offering condolences?
My colleague interrupts, asks to use the AC remote.
I want to say I don't understand the question.
Admin has emailed a request for early contract renewal.

My colleague takes the AC remote, heads for the door.
My school director leans against the doorway.
Admin has emailed a request for early contract renewal,
but that's not why he's here. He says Trump is in the lead.

My school director is Canadian.
We could shoot the breeze about anything on any day,
but that's not why he's here. *Trump is in the lead,* he says.
My colleague who has taken the AC remote is Jordanian.

We could shoot the breeze about anything, on any day.
Trust me, we can go on like this forever.
My colleague who has taken the AC remote, the Jordanian,
turns around, says: *What do you think about this man?*

Trust me, I say: *We can go on about him forever.*
But the school has a shortage of AC remotes.
What I think about this man
is the last thing on my mind,

especially when I know AC remotes are in high demand.
Abdulrahman lingers. His retelling still an open end,
and patience is the last thing on his mind.
My wife tells me everyone is offering condolences.

I want to say I don't get the joke.
I want to ask: *Who died?*

Pantoum

Let us believe for a moment that
in this poem there is no suffering,
and the white sheet is still freshly folded,
tucked away inside a dimly lit ambulance, because

in this poem there is no suffering,
and the boy wearing his hood is enjoying his Skittles,
tucked away inside a dimly lit ambulance, because
he is receiving a generous ride home.

And the boy wearing his hood is enjoying his Skittles
next to the young man from St. Louis.
He is receiving a generous ride home
as well. Paramedics are joking with the boy wearing his hood

next to the young man from St. Louis.
One says: *What do you call a freshly folded white sheet?*
Paramedics are joking with the boy wearing his hood
as another man enters the ambulance. He overhears as

one says: *What do you call a freshly folded white sheet?*
The joke is interrupted
as another man enters the ambulance. He overhears as
the paramedic repeats the question.

The joke is interrupted.
A young lady enters, says she wouldn't be caught dead for failing to signal.
The paramedic repeats the question.
A twelve-year-old boy asks for a ride. He sits down next to

the young lady who said she wouldn't be caught dead for failing to signal.
She whispers the answer to
the twelve-year-old boy who asked for a ride.
He says: *I know the answer,*

whispers the answer, too.
Let us believe, for a moment, that.

The Necessity of Poetry

after Charles Simic

God made the mosquito so men would not be idle.
Cats are habitual like siestas in Spain.

I think more about people when they are gone.
I guess in some strange way that makes me a historian.

I'm told it takes a split second for butterflies to flap their wings.
Even less for a crocodile to bat its eyes, then it's over.

If a mosquito crosses the street, I will not ask his intentions.
For he knows in absolute he is as good as dead.

My wife's eyes are sometimes a hint of sunflower,
they lie still near the ocean without distinction.

In this I learn lives are coral-reefed in reason.
Sometimes they marble into dilated moons.

Sundays are repetitious like greetings in Arabic.
I will spare you any humor of *shokolatah* and *haleeb.*
[chocolate; milk]

Somewhere between the Atlantic and God-knows-where,
my black body metastasized into thick globs of goo.

I sprouted wings, shed my legs, my sickle cell anemia,
and became a mosquito presence in far off lands.

Here, every man carries along sweat and racket.
He waves it, and every name becomes Aim and Fire.

The average honeybee beats its wings 270 times per second,
roughly six lightning bolts striking the earth with its vein.

Six babies are born globally every 240 minutes.
A bullet travels 900 meters per second—aimed at you, times two—

Never once did I explain to the child why he's dying—
why his mosquito presence fell to earth like dry rain.

If Amichai were alive, he'd say:

I watched you grow into sunflower,
mature to age of bar mitzvah, develop in oblong
twitterpations—seal it with a kiss.

Then I'd see you in the street. Eyes like stop
signs, bleached red from war.

On His way to Jerusalem, Jesus, being hungry,
sees a tree without fruit—curses it.

In its unpreparedness,
it withers away.

Underneath the shade trees of Europe,
refugees wait for bread and country.

I join them trailside, sit up into the wee hours
of the night to recount old memories in the faces of card decks:

Oh yeah, now that Sandra—Sandra was a pure queen of hearts.
Tamir—Tamir was my ace. Big Mike—now that joker was cool as hell.

And as day breaks over our flightless bodies, we rise
like static balls I touched in museums as a child.

ZEINA HASHEM BECK

the Days don't stop

the Tyrants sleep like gods
the Diplomats regret
the Diplomats are at their dinner tables
the Dancers dance
the Baker bakes the Bread rises
the Earth orbits
the Mothers weep
the Fathers weep
the Children walk in their coats
the Children know
a law against killing people in houses
is not the same as not killing people in houses
the Rain drops
the Poet writes the dead
City's name
the dead City remains dead open
like a cow hung in the cold of the slaughterhouse
the Lovers touch
the Singers sing
the Nightmares know
dreaming of being buried under the rubble
is not the same as being buried under the rubble
the Morning comes
the Bookkeepers count the Deaths & Births
the holy Book says
whoever does an atom's weight of good will see it
& whoever does an atom's weight of evil will see it
O eternal Cinematographer
the Deeds flicker
on the screens of Hell & Heaven
the fallen building keeps falling
the Saved have no Peace
the tides of Blood & Hope eat the body like a disease
O Lord please do not heal us

BRUCE BENNETT

America in 2015

after Shelley, England in 1819

A monster Egotist who thinks he's God,
A dozen jerks who fawn and test the wind
In hopes that one of them will get the nod,
Fanatics who don't care if someone sinned
So long as his comportment isn't odd
And he is armed and one of them, Truth spinned
Till it is barely truth, a people dazed
By lies that no one calls a lie, in awe
Of wealth and hype, so terrified and crazed
That they can hardly wait to flout the law
If that might harm their neighbor and keep out
Those they deem different who may get to vote;
All these, My Country, as we peer ahead
Alarmed, and face the coming year with dread!

The Lake Isle of Anywhere

I will arise and go now, and go where I am free
From tweets and lies and riots and ads and red-faced men
Who boast and taunt and argue and harp on "Me. Me. Me."
I'd rather be some creature who lives out in a fen.

For I would have some peace there, and never have to face
A mob of angry bigots who raise their fists and bray
About their loss of freedom and insults to their race
With cries of "He's Our Hero" and chants of "USA!"

I will arise and go now, for always I can hear
The frogs and gnats and crickets and little peaceful coos
Of little peaceful creatures who are not filled with fear
And do not live with loathing, because there is no news.

ROSEBUD BEN-ONI

And All the Songs We Are Meant To Be

The canon is a myth
The canon never stops evolving
The canon is otherworldly at a young age
The canon is a wind which goes against itself
The canon is a youth resisting herself
The canon is most definitely female
But answers to an exponential she
Whom within all our pain rings out differently
Because that is yours
And that is mine and we divide
And we divide
By green mile and Green Line
And rivers we make serve as soldiers
We dump and embitter and drain
There are faces in the river I have seen
There are deserts in the river I have crossed
There are prayers otherworldly at a young age
There are flames burning longer than eight days
And I'd give them away
I'd give all the land away
Just to free all the miraculous melody and din
Just to hear Jerusalem answering
To that exponential she
Imagine Jerusalem as she was meant to be
Not of one canon
Not of one anything
Imagine all the songs
And all the songs ringing across Jerusalem all the mosques
And all the churches all the synagogues
The Kotel and Dome of the Rock
All those prayers gathering
Into one another
At St. Anthony's Monastery all the chapels all the streets
Where women and men
Where women and men

Pray together and no soldiers
Appear only in ancient songs only in remembrance
And the young will say war is a myth we made up
To compel them to use their science
And extend the life of the ancient ones
When my body too is broken and resisting itself
When my body is a canon
Blowing against itself
This body we were meant to resist
This body we were meant to leave
This body an exodus
What then would be what then
If no land and no land belonged to one star
Pinned higher in the sky by jealous eyes
What then if I knew your prayers
And you knew mine
Sacred as the doorposts and gates that bind
All the songs ringing across and beyond Jerusalem
All agnostics and nonbelievers too
Have their songs and we listen
Miracles are the science unlocking the din
Scientist and poet and galactic
Historian all of kin
And no guns
And only space runs
And the table full
Minus one
Who is always late
Who drifts in the empathy of whales
Who speaks no nation but the expanse
Of open waters
In which the ancients swim
Who fears what had happened in my time
Is nothing more than a children's fable
Who wants me to take seriously
How otherworldly
She was meant to be
And who will ask me to sing my sonorous antiquity
And who will say to me, ancient one, the table is waiting

BRIAN BRODEUR

Self-Portrait with Alternative Facts

I was never born—
  I subsist
on rain and iron
  deposits
lodged in public land
  as I bore
into the ground, blind.
  Like amber,
I confine caught life:
  a canker within
an Eocene leaf.
  Whittled thin,
I needle
  toward the surface,
earth-addled,
  the spike of my face
beginning to crown
  through gravel
I claim as my own—
  the stripped vale,
the fractured
  asphalt,
the last word.
  Who could fault
the house fire
  for warming the night?
The noose for
  the dead man, his note?
I know I exist
  because I
obstruct all exits.
  I deny
my blood, resist
  like a swollen tick—
all the rest
  is myth, politics.

Lullaby for an Autocrat

"One by one, in every booth, the naphtha jets were turned down
and the canvases pulled over the little gaming tables."
—Dylan Thomas, "After the Fair"

Who but an after-hours guest
would notice, snagged in grass, the flit
of popped balloons displayed like flags
of fallen cities: Babylon
and Ugarit? Who'd pat the head

of a dozing lion, underfed,
and clap away the haloing
of gnats above its jangling tags?
Who'd prowl beneath the brown bat's flight
to peep the bearded lady's breasts?

Relax. The fairground tents, beset
by shadows, burst with straw crushed flat
as turnstiles click and moonlight drags.
Be seated now, be still, and lean
on bounce-house walls not yet deflated.

Don't fret what So-and-So has stated,
how awful much you feel alone.
Ignore the mounting garbage bags,
the naphtha jets that immolate
the carousel. You need your rest—

Sleep tight and dream these wooden beasts
run-through with poles stampede the light
that inches toward the oil-soaked rags
you bunch as pillows. Loaf, recline
and hug for warmth your burning bed.

Transcontinental

Your safety is important to us, drones
the automated voice. Our seatbelts click
like vertebrae. The cabin dims. *All phones
and portable devices*—It's a shtick,
but I admire the lexicon of flight,
the clarity and lack of condescension
in demonstrations of the brace position
and where to find our life-vests, how they fit.

Cruising in reverse, we leave the gate,
conducted by the flares of semaphores
to idle on the tarmac where we'll get
what we paid for: transference, *metaphor,*
a bag of nuts and room to stow a purse.
As seatmates locate commonalities
in brands of Yoga mats and herbal teas,
I scroll through Twitter feeds. The Airbus purrs.

Our conversations range from Netflix shows
to Trump. A woman laughs: "Why *not* embrace
the lie that saying something makes it so?"
A guy across the aisle says he still prays
before he flies. He smiles, says Facebook likes
are economic acts and he believes
Eternal Darkness 2 changed his kids' lives.
Beyond our heads, the ATCT blinks.

A flight attendant lingers by my leg—
"Your phone, sir, *please.*" What if I forget
to power-down? Would the whole fuselage
crush like an empty Coke can, conflagrate?
Preparing for our slog across the night,
the turbine engines hum in unison
the wheezy white-noise whining of their song.
Outside, the stars—trick candles—reignite.

Joel Brouwer

Some Varieties of Political Activism

The visiting dissident poet offered
our seminar a paradox. When a regime
cloaks its crimes in empty formulae
of collectivism, by what rhetoric shall
the citizenry collectively resist?
We had to ponder that one. Was there
a way to answer truthfully without
having to be honest? The edge of my cookie
grew mushy where it abutted the clutch
of wet grapes on my napkin. Earlier
we'd entertained our guest with an outing
to Dollar General. Its cleaning products
and plastics pulsed orange and green and purple,
vivid as a dish of revolutionary
sherbet. To demonstrate capitalist
vacuity (OK, we'll admit it, also
just for fun), we held up one item after
another—spatula set, cinnamon
candle in a jar, sand pail—and asked
our poet to guess: How much? How much? How much?
Despots understand how to be both
omnipresent and invisible. In the DPRK
Kim's picture hangs in every room; Hoxha
had at least four secret bunkers.
Who teaches these guys this stuff? Are there despot
seminars offered somewhere? The poet
proffered the answer we'd predicted.
Ironically, individualism
and subjectivity become the only
viable modes of general resistance!
I thought of a throng of protesters
in a rainy central square, each under
his own little umbrella. That's a lot
of umbrellas! I hope they had a way
to buy a bunch in bulk. One dollar, one

dollar, one dollar. What a joy to have
an answer that's always at hand and never
wrong. For the Skeptics it was epokhé,
suspension of assent. Blind bats careened
the twilit parking lot, symbolically
devouring the sighted bugs too dumb to
shut up, and a few Hispanic guys, framed
by the seminar room's picture window,
blew shrub cuttings to the gutter. You've heard
folks say everything looks like a nail if
you're a hammer, but what if you're a nail?
For my final project I proposed
the U. N. issue everyone a bullhorn
with which they might amplify their subjectivities.
I'm not sure I understood
the assignment. We sent the dissident
back to her country with a swag bag of
ice cube trays, room freshener, and canned milk,
and later learned that one blogger liked this.

NICKOLE BROWN

Inauguration Day, 2017

Like that horse, how sick he was
but not so sick he could not walk.

And because he was big—nearly seventeen
hands—alive or dead he could not be carried,

so my friend who loved him best
had a hole torn from her pasture deep enough

to expose the reddest dirt, the kind that refuses
new water but holds still what seeps from below.

Then with great reins she eased him
into that grave. To understand, know this:

how his eyes went before his legs, how quickly
she had to scurry out once his gaze

lost focus and glazed, quickly before his knees gave
and all that proud weight slumped and crushed her

into the dark. Know that. And know this:
this is not a metaphor for another January day

but a swallow of the same obscene
grief, a sickening hush.

You see, the horse trusted her.
No one but her could have coaxed him

into that pit with its sticky, rust-colored clay.
Know how she was forced to stay calm

so the horse would not die
afraid.

Trump's Tic Tacs

"I better use some Tic Tacs just in case I start kissing her.... I just start kissing them. It's like a magnet. Just kiss. I don't even wait. And when you're a star, they let you do it. You can do anything."

The night after my country loaded you
into its chamber and cocked
that long gun aimed straight for my
home, my wife and I were stuck
in a nearly dystopian line of unmoving
traffic. And because sugar comforts her
she popped those half-calorie candies
into her mouth and was bound to eat
the whole box herself until she shook out
from that hard plastic case the oranges ones,
just for me.

You see, Donald, this good woman,
she loves me. And she knows how the taste
of artificial orange makes me feel—
safe—makes me remember fevers broken
by the chalk tangerine of baby aspirin,
cool rags upon me, and a soft knock
on my door saying, *Baby, don't get up;
mama's just checking on you again.*
That was back when another man
not so unlike you was insecure enough
to also think it best to freshen himself before
grabbing at me, and to this day
I don't remember much except: *Don't worry.
I took a shower; it's clean.*

Donald, the news coming through the radio
made me sick. We had to turn it off.
We drove in stand-still, bumper-to-bumper
silence, unable to speak, especially not
of you. Yet there you still were,
a rattling under my tongue—those three orange

candies now tiny bullets, pills with a powdery zest
that never really were tasty but just mindless, addictive
in that high chemical way, not doing a damn thing
to sweeten anyone's breath. I could not spit
and could not swallow and helpless
let it dissolve in my mouth.

Avocado a la Ionesco

for Greg Pardlo

We didn't want to be rhinoceri   to have thick skin   or to have

to thicken it   we didn't want to be of indeterminate color   didn't want

to turn on each other   into each other   or be forced to be swept up

by forces we didn't want   to put a ring on it   didn't want

to cash it all in   to carry hot sauce in our bags   or to pretend

What we wanted   was avocados   to put on the ugly truths

to make each green but perishable   artisanal yet inclusive

to use avocados   like they use full breasts   to call attention

to the thing   we want addressed   for our plight is not pornography

Cortney Lamar Charleston

Feeling Fucked Up

after Etheridge Knight
for Walter Scott

Lord, they done did the damn deed again   took him out
like   *POOF* like ace   *BOOM*   *COON* like   *WAP* like
motherfucker   he might've been kin you know? like I'm saying
neither of us can   could run for shit   guess a cop's shot ain't
gotta be worth spit if he gets eight of them   damn   just ate shrimp
now   it's everywhere   it's dark outside my window America
is everywhere look   this brother   ain't coming back none of them
coming back turn yours on a coward they'll prove who they really
are   scared of   is you telling me I went four long-ass days
without knowing he died   that I got my tail light fixed the same
damn day he faded out in broad daylight after getting stopped
for a broken tail light? did I drop $275 just to keep living my
got-damned life?!   I got work in the a.m. but what for? who
I'm feeding? Walter Scott have kids or not? they caught them
bastards on tape   planting the Taser   next to a body
handcuffed to its own color to lifelessness itself   motherfucker
I can't even   I need a woman   to hold me tonight a good
woman like she would bury me with her own hands good if
I bit the bullet kicked the bucket of blood over I   need Jesus
some Kanye *College Dropout*   tonight I   really need
some   liquor for them to stay outta my face with all
their *oh my God!* every day they kill my God just a little bit
more believe that my brother it took a camera for all
y'all to believe this was possible but   why?   still   ain't enough
why?   my background check clean like   *tabula rasa* like you
can be white on black and free black on anything   and
dead   in jail for life *sick dopeness*   I got it don't worry   fuck it
I got it cable news is gonna have field days with this one
and the next man fuck that   if I'm being completely honest

fuck every Facebook "like" on that video fuck every share
and stock that goes up tomorrow fuck the NRA fuck elephants

and donkeys and trees fuck all the primaries and the general
fuck another White House press conference fuck every
bald-headed bird in the sky fuck "democracy" fuck oligarchy
fuck racism fuck sexism fuck heterosexism fuck classism fuck
the police state fuck law and order if that's what it takes
fuck the drug of war fuck the war on drugs fuck good
people going quiet fuck pure evil fuck the part of me that wants to
forget fuck forgetting fuck not forgetting fuck death fuck my life
fuck every single thing in sight till we all make it all   right.

Chillary Clinton Said "We Have to Bring Them to Heal"

I mean, I think that's what she was saying, right?
So how about it then? My hands are soft and ready

for work. Bring me all your sick-and-tireds, all your
bodies bruised all over, it would seem, from birth itself.

Bring me buckets of fried chicken, both original and
extra crispy. Bring me pork chops and racks on racks

of ribs. I need six-packs ad infinitum. Juice boxes
and boxes full of bagged ice. Get me circular tables,

folding chairs, old white robes to use as tablecloths,
and one full deck of cards for every set of seats: I'm

throwing a grand old party! Yes, Beyoncé is invited.
Kanye West is invited. I'm sorry if it disappoints you,

but you must understand that my mans needs to heal
with his fellow men, with women who have been hurt

by the things men have done to them, or said, or didn't say
or didn't mean to from the dustiest corners of their hearts.

Harm happens, but for what apologies and forgivenesses
never come or word alone can't communicate completely

or correctly, we invented music; bring me plastic crates
of vinyls. Turntables. Bring me speakers, power strips,

extension cords. Tell everybody coming to load their
trunks with cheap fireworks. Tell them to bring dishes

we can dole out. Solo cups. Plates and utensils. Pillows,
since we're going until moonrise at minimum, moving

the crowd, shaking our groove thangs yeah yeah. This
is a party, damn it! And I know somebody will probably

make a jackass out of themselves, but that's all part of
the experience. Somebody will drink too much, but we

won't let them drive. Somebody's cousin will say some
reckless shit and have to get put in line: that's how it goes.

It might get loud around here, but that's just because we'
all alive. Blood-wired. We dance-battled death and won.

Then we talked about it. Then we cried about it. We tried.
We tried. We tried: everybody's hands on everybody else.

Postmortem: 11/9/16

for the hyphenated and addendummed

I am not yet dead but have been dying
at an unknown speed for some time
and so I have already made peace
with the end of anything. I am not sad
or surprised, but am growing indifferent
toward those who are indifferent toward
me, loving them passively and maybe
stupidly from a distance keeping us both
safe in our own minds, though one of us
is lying the way they are dying unknowingly.

Were it not for the anthem before the game
and my muscles refusing to forget, I may not
have found a heartbeat at all, which I took as
a sign I should live, abstain attention to the
red stain on my shirt that will, at some point,
dry, though maybe not before these beautiful
bones that have framed my entire existence.

JIM DANIELS

Raking, Pittsburgh
November 9, 2016

I'm biking to work, my breath
swirling and disappearing behind me
when I see Tom and Tom sees me.

He is raking leaves. We pretend
not to see each other. We are not
ready to see each other. Raking

leaves over cement, screeching
rake against concrete, bowing
its teeth with pressure.

He's wearing his white Carhartt
overalls. Soon he will be driving
off in his yellow van to drywall

or plaster inside a house
in our fair city in a world
that seems so unfair today

that we cannot look at each
other. We are not violent men.
Yesterday, we stood in line

together and voted. We talked
about our children. We caught up.
He asked about my wife's cancer.

Today I am on my way to teach.
To pretend for eighty minutes that
at least my soul is intact. It is too soon.

It is too late. Tom and I are in
the same boat. Today we cannot
imagine that boat is not sinking.

I am speaking for Tom
because he is busy raking.
I am not sure he really needs

to rake. He appears to be
rounding up leaves that
want to blow away down the street.

We are not good at pretending,
but it's all we've got this morning.
We are not violent men.

But oh, those leaves, today.

Half-Mast

I I I you they us he he she it shit pledge ledge edge I I he flag lag gag laf gaf states asset stat teats ass as a me me me rica stands sands dans sad as sad God dog God dog gone just ick 4 all I ?

Some people think the number 13 is unlucky or that America is the greatest country in the world or that the Bible is the word of God and must be taken literally at all times and toilet paper must be unrolled from the top not the bottom and we all gotta start counting our syllables so we can leave em for our children and grandchildren and slaves and oops did I say slaves I meant bankers I meant no new taxes I meant it's eleventeen o'clock and where are your damn children? Hope they're not doing any fun stuff gun stuff bang banging on the door of infamy the women and chillen go last how's that working out for you yelling at people for playing flag football in the rocket's red glare love it or which ones are white and which read? My way or the highway nearest you does godblessamerica mean fuckeverybodyelse? but you gotta say it while wearing your lapel pin can you I heart america and still heart everybody else too or does the lapel pin prevent wearing your heart on your sleeve and what does it mean to write a poem shaped like a flag and please don't kick my ass america.

KYLE DARGAN

Americana

The last thing my vision grazes
                    ahead a red-eye
                    London departure—
Obama's smiling face on toilet paper
                    rolls pyramid-stacked
                    at the gift shop
entryway. This is Washington-Dulles
                    in his final year atop
                    a tiring administration.
I lost a good friend over the vote
                    this country cast
                    in 2008. She believed
the moment to be revolutionary. I dissented
                    that no radical seed
                    had taken root
on our soil. Had I known she and I
                    would—over that—
                    wither as friends,
I could have feigned exuberance, imitated
                    upheaval. Now, nagging
                    unemployment
statistics have since been tamed, as well as
                    the white digits
                    between the dollar sign
and the gallon. Nevertheless, eight years later,
                    some things—some friendships—
                    have not been restored.
Still, you do not see me wishing for the means
                    with which to scour
                    the President's grayscale face
against my anus. The post-wipe sarcasm—*Thanks,*
                    Obama—as a gesture
                    of the body

cleansing the body. Though didn't he run
               to clean and change
               a soiled nation's bottom?
And even that, the privilege of allowing
               someone else
               to wipe your ass,
this country could not receive from his brown
               hand housed
               in a white glove.
Twice, I have gripped the President's bare hand—
               America's shit pressed
               against my palm—
and asked him, silently, *was it worth it?* Tonight,
               I cross the Atlantic
               having lost
my antecedent for that it. Maybe just eight
               years of static. A ratcheting
               whir akin to that noise
I always hear (do you?) as the plane taxis
               towards liftoff,
               but I never bother
asking what is that sound when the pilot and I
               come face-to-face
               as we all deplane—
having jetted across time, finding ourselves
               towed only by anticipation
               of the baggage we do claim.

Mountebank

Let us commemorate his ascendancy
with a sale. How else to appreciate
a great retail politician, how to valuate
history? A Sale Unprecedented. A national
day of big-box store therapy. (Nothing
cyber. There are rarely peddlers
behind the pixel arrays.) Let us celebrate
proper the talents of salesmen—
this toolkit forgotten among recent days.
Be not mistaken. It isn't a command
of product jargon, not a graceful
demonstration of the merch. A salesman
makes you feel triumphant about
trading your coin, about the chance
to be purchaser. No pressure to confess
that buying a piece of hate wrapped
in the common red felt good (or better,
at least, than the angst of not knowing
what your pale tender will be
able to buy you in five years, or two
or tomorrow). Whether or not it was
shrewd to shell-out for this Uncle Sam's
club membership, you won't care
once these great deals cross your eyes.
Low-cost swastikas. Free hijabs
pulled right from the heads of living
models. Free delivery, free returns
of those who no longer serve
your sense of nationhood. Too good
to be true this promotion. Though
we've already bought all we need,
can't we buy again to be better
consumers, good citizens? Open
your wallet. Show respect for our once
in a lifetime tycoon—he who didn't
fabricate these synthetic flags we wave
but was savvy enough to silkscreen
his name in the white space between bars,
stars, and sell each for triple markup.
Don't you feel satisfied? How could you not
be convinced it's still a steal?

DANIELLE CADENA DEULEN

American Curse

May dark soldiers lead you through the mountains.
May you find the criminal weeping in his hands.
May the scent of whiskey rise from your horses.
May you build your mansion in the sands.

May the beauty of your children be too great for kindness.
May the forest reappear when you close your eyes.
May your dogs grow wild as your heart goes tame.
May your bullet always meet with its aim.

On the Uncertainty of Our Judgment

Oil darkens the river upstream. Another spill, another assurance from our mayor that the water is fine; he drinks a glass of it for the press, their cameras swallow it up. But *purely as a precautionary measure*, he's shut down the river water intakes, let the city draw from its reservoirs—or someone has, some water works worker, I imagine, in a grey jumpsuit,

two days' growth of hair on his pale face, stinking of loneliness. Everything remains the same since Monday's spill, my breasts leaking milk onto my sheets, onto the face of my half-lidded baby when I jerk myself awake, asleep, awake, up on my bare feet in the bathroom where the toilet leaks, smells faintly of piss, but in my stupor I keep stepping into puddles,

forgetting, distracted, my baby already (I can hear him) stirring. I turn on the faucet. Somewhere deep beneath my house, old lead service lines pull the water up to me, where it burns over my hands. *White lead*, as described in *Alexipharmaca* of Nicander: *gleaming, deadly, whose fresh colour is like milk, which foams all over.* That slight sting my nipples make

before the *let down* begins, but my baby is sleeping. Is he sleeping? Maybe he's just calm, waiting to open his eyes, little planet. Last night's storm has escaped his gaping mouth. The fists he shook at the walls are limp now, would slip easily over the rail of his crib like a tiny bow, rise with the music in his dreams, which swell and turn— dark clouds beneath his lids.

No one knows how far the spill has traveled since it entered the river, if the water has already sluiced the fuel downstream into our pipelines. But we have assurances. *What's important here is to recover our losses*, says the mayor, meaning *the oil*, which he has ordered the Coast Guard to vacuum out of the water so it might still be bought and sold. This is a value system not much different from Greece of 15 BC, when Vitruvius wrote about the dangers of commonplace poison. He described the lead workers as having *a pallid colour; the fumes from daily casting destroyed the vigour of the blood*. But lead was abundant, malleable, with a low melting point—it was easy, everywhere. So the ancients used it to shape and solder pipes, sweeten sour wine,

line their aqueducts, transport live fish in tanks made from it, knowing its effect on the body. At this hour, there's almost silence: the metronome of the mechanical swing rocking my boy, the throated note he suckles down. Why do I imagine that water works worker to be lonely? Perhaps he's walking toward the valve intake now, imagining applause, whistling a jaunty tune,

inexplicably happy in the black morning while I hum my boy archaic lullabies, wondering if a mother's body can filter out bad water, make it sweet. I may be going mad from lack of sleep. Or perhaps it's lead in the blood—*Saturnism*, after the planet god, who orbited slowly, but erupted in violence or revelry. I'm trying to teach my son a wariness I don't abide by—the wound

just sutured shut beneath my belly where he was lifted out of me, chord noosed around his neck, into a surgical room, the lights tined around us, the silver instruments, physicians spiraling, shouting, making their assurances. When I asked what was wrong, they set my shivering newborn on my chest as if he were an answer. Should I wake him now, press

a burning nipple into his mouth, let him drain my aching breast? From outside a light brightens then seeps from his face. *It will pass*, the mayor says in every conference with the press. *It will pass*. Rising toward my son sleeping beneath the window, I feel dizzy, brace myself against the pane, my hand on the glass, wondering how hard I'd have to press to break through.

We Are Bored

So we line our bottles on the fence and aim, or swim
into the river's gullet, let it swallow us bare—the vellum
sheen of mud on our skin. We drive for hours into
the wind, chasing last light and a time before toil, stage
a breakdown, strike a flare just to see who pulls over.
We blindfold and spin each other around, assault piñatas
with blunt sticks, heat the flesh of a hog in a pit—
charcoal and dirt—until we can pull its eyes from its face.
We get so lit we stagger across the sky. We burn
our cigars, the dense scent of burning loam sucked
down our throats, our lungs shuddering like dying
birds, or we trace our shadows, punch the air, rub
welts into each other's arms, pull off our clothes,
climb into back seats, press our mouths against windows
to write our names on glass. We pluck the bright faces
of flowers, stick our fists into hives to steal the afterglow.
We build forts from bed sheets to hide in, kiss, slap each
other's faces, tour the periphery of abandoned buildings.
We follow the sound of sirens away from the suburbs
into the thrumming cities, crowd on the sidewalks to
watch medics pulling the bodies away. We dare each other
into graveyards to fuck against tombstones, walk out
into traffic, change our names, quit our jobs, migrate
to other cities, tattoo ourselves with the names of lovers
who will try to forget us. We jump out of airplanes,
earth as open as an eye as we fall irrevocably toward it.
We pound our fists on the hoods of cars, stare into
the blazing fires we've set, light dynamite in the open fields
just to see how fast we can run. We wrestle with the ghosts
of our fathers, look so long at constellations we see
our faces in them. We break into factories, winnow
crowbars into the turbines, throw bricks through the sooted
windows, set the goddamn things on fire. We rush into
the revival tent to swoon into salvation, handle the serpents,
prove we are pure, we are holy. We talk in tongues, pierce
our nipples, drive ink-guns into our shoulders, slam a bat
into the clerk's face, gamble the house away, give our money
to God, incite riots we have no intention of stopping, rev
our engines at stoplights, drag razors over the soft inside

of thighs, sink into bathtubs, kneel in pews, kneel in alleys,
kneel closed-eyed on the filthy mattress, light the pipe,
lie to our families, invent past lovers, divorce our wives
just to marry them again, denounce our children,
then ask their forgiveness. We dance wildly in the arms
of strangers, swallow another handful of pills, throw
a wedding party where the groom is unfettered and where,
already, the bride is crying. We drink champagne and eat
our cake too, throw a ball into the grandstand, roll a joint,
spike the punch, conceive a child who will hate us.
We write poems, run red lights, get so lost in the forest
we nearly starve. We go to the office with three shotguns
and a bomb. We look for weapons of mass destruction,
confess to prostitutes, tell stories to lawyers. We swallow
amphetamines to work through the night, go into
the mountains to learn from the sky. We run for no reason
in the split-light morning, go down to the jail to steal
the prisoners, hang them from sycamores, telephone polls.
We stab a flag into the chest of the moon, keep watching
the screen though it only shows static. We march through
the streets to show our medals, toss up confetti, pitch
hard candies at children, we beat our drums, shine our
trumpets, twirl batons so high they seem to matter, walk
deep into the desert to watch the bomb go off, to watch it
grow and grow like a backwards cloud rooted from dunes.
We speculate on how we can use it: for love, entertainment,
profit, the poor. We can use it to prove our strength, use it
for the war we never want to end, the war we keep starting,
the unkempt war with its mouth gaping, with its fists against
the caves like a monstrous, vacant child, the sun cracking
our skin, the sandstorms blasting our faces open. We let
the heat wilt our minds as we wander back into the suburbs,
beneath the wan streetlights, beyond the cul-de-sac's end.
We whittle our names into the trunks of pines, which harrow
us with the way they stand so still under the sun and rain,

never feeling the slow rot of the heart, never waking to
the light of their failures, never lying down across the steel
rails of the trellis the way we do just to feel the weight of
the iron beneath us, the damp air rising up from the river
through the blank, splintered wood, and that long, slow
moan deep in our bones—the call of the oncoming train.

NATALIE DIAZ

Post-Colonial Love Poem

I've been taught bloodstones can cure a snakebite,
can stop the bleeding—most people forgot this
when the war ended. The war ended
depending on which war you mean: those we started,
before those, millennia ago and onward,
those which started me, which I lost and won—
these ever-blooming wounds.
I was built by wage. So I wage Love and worse—
always another campaign to march across
a desert night for the cannon flash of your pale skin
settling in a silver lagoon of smoke at your breast.
I dismount my dark horse, bend to you there, deliver you
the hard pull of all my thirsts—
I learned Drink in a country of drought.
We pleasure to hurt, leave marks
the size of stones—each a cabochon polished
by our mouths. I, your lapidary, your lapidary wheel
turning—green mottled red—
the jaspers of our desires.
There are wild flowers in my desert
which take up to twenty years to bloom.
The seeds sleep like geodes beneath hot feldspar sand
until a flash flood bolts the arroyo, lifting them
in its copper current, opens them with memory—
they remember what their god whispered
into their ribs: Wake up and ache for your life.
Where your hands have been are diamonds
on my shoulders, down my back, thighs—
I am your culebra.
I am in the dirt for you.
Your hips are quartz-light and dangerous,
two rose-horned rams ascending a soft desert wash
before the November sky unyokes a hundred-year flood—
the desert returned suddenly to its ancient sea.
Arise the wild heliotrope, scorpion weed,

blue phacelia which hold purple the way a throat can hold
the shape of any great hand—
Great hands is what she called mine.
The rain will eventually come, or not.
Until then, we touch our bodies like wounds—
the belled bruises fingers ring
against the skin are another way to bloom.
The war never ended and somehow begins again.

DANTE DI STEFANO

National Anthem with Elegy and Talon

Looking at the North Star this February
evening, I can feel the word "father" pulse
down my jugular vein and hibernate
in the phalanxes of my finger bones.
"Father," vellum whispers to the bull-god
in the pasture. Call this lowing, religion.
"Father," apple mouths as it scuds to earth.
Every sad thing in the human heart weighs
the sum of dust motes dancing in sunlight.
Call this truth the portage and redemption
of a childhood memory alchemized
into bramble and ash. There, my mother
remains locked in the basement, a barbell-
shaped bruise throbbed tuberous under her blouse.
"Father," the rusting bayonet rumors
to the plastic-wrapped full dress uniform
starched on a hanger in the bomb shelter;
its sharpshooter medals shine like astral
doubloons a-glimmer in the galleon
of a distant nebula's wrecked outline.
Here in America, trauma and rage
dovetail, become birthright, counterclaim us;
the wind brinks through plain poplar and linden,
consecrating the air above your grave.
Your face was always etched like a tombstone,
I say to the mirror in the morning,
and there you are, my father, a bequest
of crow's feet in an era of warring
tribes and constellations, and brilliant claws.

celeste doaks

American Herstory

Tell them it's always under attack. Tell them there's no cure
for the disease, or answer to the riddle. Tell them you asked many
before you, some who won, some who lost.

You consulted Assata, Roe vs. Wade, Harriet and Joycelyn Elders
to no avail. Her words on contraception twisted into a bitter pretzel.
The bits broken off, used to destroy her.

Tell them it's always under attack, its predators everywhere. They lurk
behind Mississippi clinics or around Georgetown blocks dressed
in blue uniform. Tell them you have the cure, somewhere at home,

deep in your cabinets, mixed in a mason jar. Don't tell them
it consists of breast milk, dreams, butterflies, civil rights marches,
burned bras, a piece of Madame CJ Walker's hair, prayers,
Amelia Earhart's drive, hot-water cornbread, and Sally Ride's fearlessness.

Lie to them, tell them it's rosemary oil, then bottle it. Sell it
to every woman in America who will drink it. Then watch all
the piranhas disappear.

How to Survive When Militants Knock at Your Door

*Dedicated to Cynthia Cherotich and the 147 Kenyans massacred
at Garissa University*

When they show up at your door, their dark
rifles staring you down, run and search for anything
that will conceal your body. Become best friends with a crawlspace
above a chifforobe. Collapse your small girlish frame
into its coffin like constraints. Pray your grandmother's cross
doesn't clang as you shiver. Cover yourself in jackets, scarves,
and white blouses for class and wait. Wait, while the machine gun dust
fills your nostrils. Wait right there while bodies thud
to the floor, watching the slow seep of red between pine planks.
You wait there for hours, then days. Drink lotion
to quench your thirst. Keep waiting. Even when
the rescuers arrive you flinch with disbelief, because
for days you have been daydreaming of butterflies
carrying you off to some garden far, far away.

MARTÍN ESPADA

How We Could Have Lived or Died This Way

> "Not songs of loyalty alone are these,
> But songs of insurrection also,
> For I am the sworn poet of every dauntless rebel the world over."
> —Walt Whitman

I see the dark-skinned bodies falling in the street as their ancestors fell
before the whip and steel, the last blood pooling, the last breath spitting.
I see the immigrant street vendor flashing his wallet to the cops,
shot so many times there are bullet holes in the soles of his feet.
I see the deaf woodcarver and his pocketknife, crossing the street
in front of a cop who yells, then fires. I see the drug raid, the wrong
door kicked in, the minister's heart seizing up. I see the man hawking
a fistful of cigarettes, the cop's chokehold that makes his wheezing
lungs stop wheezing forever. I am in the crowd, at the window,
kneeling beside the body left on the asphalt for hours, covered in a sheet.

I see the suicides: the conga player handcuffed for drumming on the subway,
hanged in the jail cell with his hands cuffed behind him; the suspect leaking
blood from his chest in the back seat of the squad car; the 300-pound boy
said to stampede barehanded into the bullets drilling his forehead.

I see the coroner nodding, the words he types in his report burrowing
into the skin like more bullets. I see the government investigations stacking,
words buzzing on the page, then suffocated as bees suffocate in a jar. I see
the next Black man, fleeing as the fugitive slave once fled the slave-catcher,
shot in the back for a broken tail light. I see the cop handcuff the corpse.

I see the rebels marching, hands upraised before the riot squads,
faces in bandannas against the tear gas, and I walk beside them unseen.
I see the poets, who will write the songs of insurrection generations unborn
will read or hear a century from now, words that make them wonder
how we could have lived or died this way, how the descendants of slaves
still fled and the descendants of slave-catchers still shot them, how we awoke
every morning without the blood of the dead sweating from every pore.

Sleeping on the Bus

How we drift in the twilight of bus stations,
how we shrink in overcoats as we sit,
how we wait for the loudspeaker
to tell us when the bus is leaving,
how we bang on soda machines
for lost silver, how bewildered we are
at the vision of our own faces
in white-lit bathroom mirrors.

How we forget the bus stations of Alabama,
Birmingham to Montgomery,
how the Freedom Riders were abandoned
to the beckoning mob, how afterwards
their faces were tender and lopsided as spoiled fruit,
fingers searching the mouth for lost teeth,
and how the riders, descendants
of Africa and Europe both, kept riding
even as the mob with pleading hands wept fiercely
for the ancient laws of segregation.

How we forget Biloxi, Mississippi, a decade before,
where no witnesses spoke to cameras,
how a brown man in military uniform
was pulled from the bus by police
when he sneered at the custom of the back seat,
how the magistrate proclaimed a week in jail
and went back to bed with a shot of whiskey,
how the brownskinned soldier could not sleep
as he listened for the prowling of his jailers,
the muttering and cardplaying of the hangmen
they might become.
His name is not in the index;
he did not tell his family for years.
How he told me, and still I forget.

How we doze upright on buses,
how the night overtakes us
in the babble of headphones,
how the singing and clapping

of another generation
fade like distant radio
as we ride, forehead
heavy on the window,
how we sleep, how we sleep.

Isabel's Corrido

Para Isabel

Francisca said: *Marry my sister so she can stay in the country.*
I had nothing else to do. I was twenty-three and always cold, skidding
in cigarette-coupon boots from lamppost to lamppost through January
in Wisconsin. Francisca and Isabel washed bed sheets at the hotel,
sweating in the humidity of the laundry room, conspiring in Spanish.

I met her the next day. Isabel was nineteen, from a village where the elders
spoke the language of the Aztecs. She would smile whenever the ice pellets
of English clattered around her head. When the justice of the peace said
You may kiss the bride, our lips brushed for the first and only time.
The borrowed ring was too small, jammed into my knuckle.
There were snapshots of the wedding and champagne in plastic cups.

Francisca said: *The snapshots will be proof for Immigration.*
We heard rumors of the interview: they would ask me the color
of her underwear. They would ask her who rode on top.
We invented answers and rehearsed our lines. We flipped through
Immigration forms at the kitchen table the way other couples
shuffled cards for gin rummy. After every hand, I'd deal again.

Isabel would say: *Quiero ver las fotos.* She wanted to see the pictures
of a wedding that happened but did not happen, her face inexplicably
happy, me hoisting a green bottle, dizzy after half a cup of champagne.

Francisca said: *She can sing corridos,* songs of love and revolution
from the land of Zapata. All night Isabel sang corridos in a barroom
where no one understood a word. I was the bouncer and her husband,
so I hushed the squabbling drunks, who blinked like tortoises in the sun.

Her boyfriend and his beer cans never understood why she married me.
Once he kicked the front door down, and the blast shook the house
as if a hand grenade detonated in the hallway. When the cops arrived,
I was the translator, watching the sergeant watching her, the inscrutable
squaw from every Western he had ever seen, bare feet and long black hair.

We lived behind a broken door. We lived in a city hidden from the city.
When her headaches began, no one called a doctor. When she disappeared
for days, no one called the police. When we rehearsed the questions

for Immigration, Isabel would squint and smile. *Quiero ver las fotos,*
she would say. The interview was canceled, like a play on opening night
shut down when the actors are too drunk to take the stage. After she left,
I found her crayon drawing of a bluebird tacked to the bedroom wall.

I left too, and did not think of Isabel again until the night Francisca called to say:
Your wife is dead. Something was growing in her brain. I imagined my wife
who was not my wife, who never slept beside me, sleeping in the ground,
wondered if my name was carved into the cross above her head, no epitaph
and no corrido, another ghost in a riot of ghosts evaporating from the skin
of dead Mexicans who staggered for days without water through the desert.

Thirty years ago, a girl from the land of Zapata kissed me once
on the lips and died with my name nailed to hers like a broken door.
I kept a snapshot of the wedding; yesterday it washed ashore on my desk.

There was a conspiracy to commit a crime. This is my confession: I'd do it again.

Jorge the Church Janitor Finally Quits

Cambridge, Massachusetts, 1989

No one asks
where I am from,
I must be
from the country of janitors,
I have always mopped this floor.
Honduras, you are a squatter's camp
outside the city
of their understanding.

No one can speak
my name,
I host the fiesta
of the bathroom,
stirring the toilet
like a punchbowl.
The Spanish music of my name
is lost
when the guests complain
about toilet paper.

What they say
must be true:
I am smart,
but I have a bad attitude.

No one knows
that I quit tonight,
maybe the mop
will push on without me,
sniffing along the floor
like a crazy squid
with stringy gray tentacles.
They will call it Jorge.

Alabanza: In Praise of Local 100

*for the 43 members of Hotel Employees and Restaurant Employees
Local 100, working at the Windows on the World restaurant,
who lost their lives in the attack on the World Trade Center*

Alabanza. Praise the cook with a shaven head
and a tattoo on his shoulder that said *Oye,*
a blue-eyed Puerto Rican with people from Fajardo,
the harbor of pirates centuries ago.
Praise the lighthouse in Fajardo, candle
glimmering white to worship the dark saint of the sea.
Alabanza. Praise the cook's yellow Pirates cap
worn in the name of Roberto Clemente, his plane
that flamed into the ocean loaded with cans for Nicaragua,
for all the mouths chewing the ash of earthquakes.
Alabanza. Praise the kitchen radio, dial clicked
even before the dial on the oven, so that music and Spanish
rose before bread. Praise the bread. *Alabanza.*

Praise Manhattan from a hundred and seven flights up,
like Atlantis glimpsed through the windows of an ancient aquarium.
Praise the great windows where immigrants from the kitchen
could squint and almost see their world, hear the chant of nations:
*Ecuador, México, República Dominicana,
Haiti, Yemen, Ghana, Bangladesh.*
Alabanza. Praise the kitchen in the morning,
where the gas burned blue on every stove
and exhaust fans fired their diminutive propellers,
hands cracked eggs with quick thumbs
or sliced open cartons to build an altar of cans.
Alabanza. Praise the busboy's music, the *chime-chime*
of his dishes and silverware in the tub.

Alabanza. Praise the dish-dog, the dishwasher
who worked that morning because another dishwasher
could not stop coughing, or because he needed overtime
to pile the sacks of rice and beans for a family
floating away on some Caribbean island plagued by frogs.
Alabanza. Praise the waitress who heard the radio in the kitchen
and sang to herself about a man gone. *Alabanza.*

After the thunder wilder than thunder,
after the shudder deep in the glass of the great windows,
after the radio stopped singing like a tree full of terrified frogs,
after night burst the dam of day and flooded the kitchen,
for a time the stoves glowed in darkness like the lighthouse in Fajardo,
like a cook's soul. Soul I say, even if the dead cannot tell us
about the bristles of God's beard because God has no face,
soul I say, to name the smoke-beings flung in constellations
across the night sky of this city and cities to come.
Alabanza I say, even if God has no face.

Alabanza. When the war began, from Manhattan and Kabul
two constellations of smoke rose and drifted to each other,
mingling in icy air, and one said with an Afghan tongue:
Teach me to dance. We have no music here.
And the other said with a Spanish tongue:
I will teach you. Music is all we have.

JOSHUA JENNIFER ESPINOZA

The Moon Is Trans

The moon is trans.
From this moment forward, the moon is trans.
You don't get to write about the moon anymore unless you respect
that.
You don't get to talk to the moon anymore unless you use her
correct pronouns.
You don't get to send men to the moon anymore unless their job is
to bow down before her and apologize for the sins of the earth.
She is waiting for you, pulling at you softly,
telling you to shut the fuck up already please.
Scientists theorize the moon was once a part of the earth
that broke off when another planet struck it.
Eve came from Adam's rib.
Etc.
Do you believe in the power of not listening
to the inside of your own head?
I believe in the power of you not listening
to the inside of your own head.
This is all upside down.
We should be talking about the ways that blood
is similar to the part of outer space between the earth and the
moon
but we're busy drawing it instead.
The moon is often described as dead, though she is very much
alive.
The moon has not known the feeling of not wanting to be dead
for any extended period of time
in all of her existence, but
she is not delicate and she is not weak.
She is constantly moving away from you the only way she can.
She never turns her face from you because of what you might do.
She will outlive everything you know.

[It is quiet in the morning.]

It is quiet in the morning.
I am female-bodied.
Last night's air is still
inside the trees.
A loud clap of thunder
from earlier this month
is stuck in the window.
I dress myself with
a large paper bag
and go outside in the wind.
Nothing happens.
I shudder
and break into pieces
but nothing happens.
You come out and find me
alone in the grass
covered in a purple rash.
You call me lacking
and kiss me with the words
that erase me from existence.
Everything I've done
comes from a place of dying.
.

.

.

.

[The woman is about hair]

The woman is about hair
gathering on the ground and between the breasts
that move up and down with each breath
in suffering.
In twenty years I will exist.
Even if I'm dead in twenty years I will exist
more than I do now.
I shave my legs in the shower
until my ass goes numb.
The water gathers all of me around
and says "that's what you get"
the same way men say
"that's just how the world works"
as if they're happy about it.
I make a prayer for you in front of the closet mirror
where the light from inside moves
around the room to see itself reflected.
The woman sees herself in everything and nothing.
You can open the news and read
anything you want to.
That's the magic of being alive here.
You can even read about yourself
long after you're dead.

BLAS FALCONER

The Promised Land

They disassembled the bed, emptied drawers, and left what they found
  no longer necessary or

too heavy, or held a memory they'd rather not carry: the small deaths,
  for example, buried in the yard.

Driving away, they didn't stop to look, not once, at the city, blinking
  in the night.

Tired after all these years and hungry for what they couldn't name,
  they passed the houses, glancing at each other, now, with new
  tenderness.

Gone was the barn with its rotting roof.

Gone the broken lock.

Gone the overgrowth, the rusted carport, the little ways one person
  can diminish another.

They'd been warned of earthquakes and traffic, but wouldn't the light
  be different there?

In the picture, blinds hung lopsided, and a tree stood in the window.

There were oranges among the leaves, some of them bright, large,
  and ready to eat.

KATE FALVEY

The Line

When the brackets—left bottom corner,
right top—filed plastically down the line, I dipped
swiftly into the glue pot and plugged
my brackets home.
No wiggle room permitted, I fixed
the cork boards in the tray.
A glut of Dudley Do-Rights.
Eight hours. Every day.

Down the line, she,
bleached hair stiff with silence, she
with scrawny breakneck reach,
was charged with right bottom corner,
left top. She trained us to exceed
the quota, to gain a preternatural speed
by tapping brackets to a beat,
to never miss a mark by dreaming on the line.

She—this Midge or Marge, Lou Ann, Loreen—
had final say and wiped the drips of errant glue away
as if precision counted. As if corkboards
ruled the world. She'd rake
her glaucous no-chance eyes
over the bush league summer help
and suck her smoker's tongue
like her mouth was slick with glue.

She'd show us what do, her words in check,
reserved for breaks with Belva, Jan, or Lyn,
her cronies in-the-know who worked the line
or stamped the cork with highly skilled
machines or even—times were changing—cut
the cork to spec. But this was rare.
Cutting went to men. As did the packing,
lifting, trucking, upper management.

Even then I knew
she hated me and Terry
passing through,
and our airy college giggles
and our nerve
for being young,
for not sticking to our place,
for swerving out of line,
while she,
the stickler boss
of cork board brackets,
would plant her swollen feet
until she fell
ensuring slabs
of cartoon printed cork
were cleanly planted
in their umber colored trays.
She'd never get away
until they closed the plant.
(which they did in '83)
Or the cancer got her.
She didn't start out mean,
we figured when we chose
to speculate.
Just lost her dreams,
her consciousness. Her fight.
Then it all became too much
and much
too late.

After each shift, my hands were scabbed
with glue—a carapace of honey red
I'd pick off through the night
and when my eyes were closed, I'd see
waves of visionary brackets filing forth
like the after image of the ebb and flow of surf
after a bland and careless day
on a ceaseless sandy beach.

We saved our paychecks,
then we split.
The next vacation we did stints
at the plastics factory in the town
where Terry lived.
I sealed plastic inserts for leather wallets
with a treadle press, and jotted moody
poems on filched cardboard on the sly.

The lady line boss had a twitchy eye
and bloated teased up hair,
the same regard for snipping plastic
with efficient picky care
as the cork boss lady did for neatly gluing brackets.
Terry and I shared jokes but were never unaware
that we were interlopers, temporary workers
and lucky to be leaving—free to leave.

Geri, Joan, Dotty, Marge, Marie—
I saw then—but with a young girl's sinews,
restlessness, unwitting condescension.
My aging bones now hum with memories
of how you stood for fifteen, twenty years
fending off imagined sneers of anyone with plenty.
Anyone with thoughts beyond a line you couldn't cross.
I see now that you have always been my boss.

BRIAN FANELLI

Post-Election

When this is over,
after we retire canvassing clipboards,
peel stickers off our coats,
remove weather-beaten yard signs,

I want to walk tree-lined streets with you,
feel the warmth of your hand coupling mine,
catch the last glimpse of Pennsylvania foliage,
canopies of remaining red and brown.

When this is over,
after a bleary-eyed Tuesday,
watching states shaded red and blue on big screens,
tossing pizza boxes and beer cans curbside,

I want to eat breakfast with you, silence our smartphones,
leave newspapers on the porch, mute morning talk shows
as I reach across the table, take your hand,
remember when we weren't headline-obsessed,

how good it felt to linger in such moments
when the sun's first rays crack the sky.

At the Corner Bar, Months Before an Election

Outside, humidity fogs our glasses, and the moon hangs,
pregnant in the sky, red like blood,
blood that colors streets of crime scenes,
during this summer of police shootings in Dallas,
preceded by black men shot, their deaths caught on cam.

Inside Rummy's corner bar,
big screen TVs blare political ads
three months before an election, ads that claim
this opponent and that opponent have closer ties
to Wall Street, ads flashing dollar signs, police batons,

or masked terrorists. Across from us, a man in a bandana claims,
Mexicans are taking it all. He pounds his PBR, while his buddy
in a gray wife beater buries his face in his hands
and then looks up to take a long drag of his cigarette,
before he says, *I'd deport them all.*

We finish our beers, unsure of election outcomes
or what else these men will say, who they'll blame
for empty factories, rows of blackened storefronts downtown,
or police shootings on nightly news.
You look to me, waiting for me to respond,
but I know anything I say will strike a match,

and their faces will blaze like a sparked cigarette,
so we leave, out into sweltering night.

Instructions for the Day After

Do not talk politics in class,
even though students stare at you
wide-eyed, like pallbearers
who just lost a relative or friend.

Years ago, in some teaching theory class,
you learned to be objective, even now,
as some shift in their seats, listening
to Hispanic DREAMers cry for their parents,

fearing that someone will kick down their door,
drag their relatives out in the middle of the night,
or the early morning, when dew kisses blades of grass
and exhaust from deportation trucks chokes the air.

You were told to be objective, even now,
when LGBT students scroll through their phones,
pull up a picture—gay man beaten, blood streaking
his face, eyes swollen, nose bashed.

Do not tell anyone that they are wrong, that not voting
can have dire consequences, as one student's hand trembles
and she pulls out a crumbled tissue, confesses
she didn't vote because the real progressive wasn't on the ballot.

Do not write political poems, not now,
because you were told as an undergrad
that political poems become dated, like rolled-up,
rain-smeared newspaper headlines, but this,

this, will never feel dated, as headlines scream
about a surprise victory, and under the A1 lead,
more headlines about hate crimes since Tuesday's results,
possible pathways to building a wall, shredding climate agreements.

Do not listen to that poetry professor who preached
from a warm classroom, inside a castle-like building,
sitting upon a tree-lined, Philadelphia suburban campus,
a time when no students feared deportation or could imagine

a time like this, when your students need to seize their pens
and know that you will listen.

ARIEL FRANCISCO

American Night, American Morning

"Fuck a dollar and a dream."
—Biggie Smalls

When I can't sleep I go
up to the rooftop
of my apartment building

and watch the man who sleeps
on the bus stop bench
across the street, brown by birth

or sun. I want to ask him
How do you do it?
From here I can see a lottery

jackpot billboard off the highway
mid-update, so that it currently reads
WIN 0 MILLION.

I was born in the city
that never sleeps so perhaps
insomnia is my birthright.

Even in Miami, the New York
air must have stuck to the inside
of my lungs like cigarette tar,

directing my luck towards
noise and lights. Sometimes
it's the cops who always

pull people over in front
of my apartment at every hour
with their howling sirens,

sometimes it's the jet planes
across the street, rattling
my windows with takeoff,

their overcaffeinated pilots
dreaming of sleep too.
Sometimes it's the stack

of mail on my nightstand
from the doctor's office,
credit card companies, Sallie

Mae, the IRS, all unopened,
collecting dust instead
of collecting from me.

The things that weigh me down
must have pressed me into sleep
right on the rooftop because I wake

to sparrows hopping about
my head, the highway singing
its blues of passing traffic.

The sun hangs in the sky
out of reach, revealing
the unfamiliar faces

at the bus stop, how much
the lottery is now, how late
I am for work.

CHRISTINE GELINEAU

Welcome: for a Grandson Born to Unsettling Times

1.

We all arrive as aliens, smeared
in our astronaut suits of vernix, trailing
our umbilicus to the old world,
gravitationally pulled to the great
magma heart of our mother.
Like every mother newly-delivered
earth welcomes the newborn to the
whole of her, heir to all her green
comforts, her silver waters, her nimbus
of air.　　　　Yet what brute sibling
forces are already deciding
what to permit, what to
deny, naming *tribe*, naming
stranger, delineating
no

2.

Not everyone will love you, Xavier,
grandson newly come, the blood
in your veins already ahum
with your ancestors' songs of exile
and hope: Greta (the great-grandmother
whose birthdate you share) Kindertransported
to London…her cousin Annelise Frank
not so fortunate; Nora of Connaught,
economic refugee; James Patrick of Tyrone,
political refugee; Herbert slipping Merzig
to Luxembourg to Le Harve to New York
just ahead of the Nazis, these matrices
of disconnection mere metonymy
of the suffering humans bring

upon one another, yes, you are born
into risk, as we all must be but born
as well into this web we create, mesh
of connection, buoyed by the many
who already do cherish you.
Grandson, inhale *home* with each bellow
of your new lungs, cry forth the sweet wail
of your own indigenous freedom song
first bell-clear note in becoming everything
your mother hopes for from you.

MARIA MAZZIOTTI GILLAN

The Day After the Election

On the day after the election,
I wake up to news I hope has to
be wrong, though I know it isn't.
Last night when I began to suspect
that Hillary would lose, I went to bed
thinking that if I went to sleep,
what looked like what was going to happen wouldn't,
but of course, it did.

I think of my father,
my radical, political father,
in love with the news and newspapers,
my father dead already 20 years.
I remember the way in 1994, when he could no longer walk,
he wanted me to take him to Washington
to march. "The American people are asleep," he said.

He'd tell me about Mussolini,
how the people fell in love with him,
how he promised that he would save them from poverty and despair.
They believed him until the Brownshirts descended on the town.
And quickly and quietly, anyone who spoke up was put in jail.
That was the end of the new dream,
the beginning of reality.

This morning, I think of my father.
I know he would've wanted to do something,
to stop what is happening to the America he so loved,
this Italian immigrant whose heroes were Roosevelt and JFK,
who believed America was the greatest country in the world.

Each day that passes,
each new cabinet appointment,
I become more and more frightened.
I hope my father is peacefully playing cards with his friends

in that heavenly grape arbor, half glasses of wine before them,
peach slices gleaming like amber in the wine.
But here on earth, each day another cabinet appointment,
people in charge of departments they hate,
responsible for programs they want to destroy.

My student says it was no choice between the two candidates
and that's why she didn't vote.
This student has no husband,
has two children,
lives on food stamps and welfare.
She writes about what it is like to be hungry.
She believes there is no difference between the two candidates.

Oh beautiful America, I am afraid. I am crying.
I don't know what we can do to help you.
Father, if you knew what happened,
if you could get out of the mausoleum drawer we filed you in,
if you could break through the steel and metal, you would
if you could, be as strong as you were when you were young,
you'd ride down to Washington to protest.
How can we lose all you believed?

I am ashamed before you, Father.
I want to turn into one of the old Italian ladies at funerals,
the ones who tore at their hair,
the ones who threw themselves into the coffins.
I'd like to be strong enough to stop what is happening.
I'd like to have your courage, Father,
and I can only hope you are sitting in sunlight
in heaven and you don't know what's happening.
America, I am crying for you.

Jennifer Givhan

The Polar Bear

> "I'm just another asshole sitting behind a desk writing about this"
> —Facebook status update

What I'm asking is will watching The Discovery
Channel with my young black boy instead
of the news coverage of the riot funerals riot arrests
riot nothing changes riots be enough to keep him
from harm? We are on my bed crying for what we've done
to the polar bears, the male we've bonded with on-screen
whose search for seals on the melting ice has led him
to an island of walruses and he is desperate, it is late-
summer and he is starving and soon the freeze
will drive all life back into hiding, so he goes for it,
the dangerous hunt, the canine-sharp tusks
and armored hides for shields, the fused weapon
they create en masse, the whole island a system
for the elephant-large walruses who, in fear, huddle
together, who, in fear, fight back. This is not an analogy.
The polar bear is hungry. The walruses fight back.
A mother pushes her pup into the icy water
and spears the hunter through the legs, the gut,
his blood clotting his fur as he curls into the ice
only feet away from the fray—where the walruses
have gathered again, sensing the threat has passed.
My boy's holding his stuffed animal, the white body
of the bear he loves, who will die tonight (who
has already died) and my boy asks me
is this real? What I'm asking is how long will we stay
walruses, he and I, though I know this is not an analogy.

The Glance

for Sunday

Through window through curtains wide through
singing after shower through racial lines and statutory
laws through landscape pebbles off the complex
path through morning's rituals before the sun could rise
through glass pane while I dreamt in our bed while our plump
brown baby slept in his slatted crib through slanted white light
through window on your way to work you heard
a song you heard a sweet song and turned your head toward
the naked girl. When the police knocked on our door.
When the police came to our door. Let me rephrase
that. When the police. They claimed you climbed
on a rock. They claimed it was a shower, the white
girl's white mother. They claimed the window
was the shower's and the window eight feet high.
They claimed you carried ladders or were made of stilts
or could form pebbles into whole rocks for climbing.
They made signs they posted on our door.
They made signs for better watch our backs.
They made signs for night watch for on guard
for dark man with Afro. After we'd moved away
after we'd hired a lawyer and the case was dropped
for lack of evidence after there was no rock
after we'd claimed the jagged edges of any safe space
we could, in Koreatown, where I daily pushed
our baby's stroller through the apartment's garden
with koi ponds past doorways that smelled of boiled
fish and our baby learned to name the things he saw
nice tree the oak with gall, the spindle wasp gall that leaves
had formed like scar tissue around the wound
where insect larva were eating their way through
the window of a neighbor's home I looked up
and watched a round man from the shower, letting
towel slip I couldn't look away from this strange
intoxicating body in front of me. We know
nothing happened after that. I took our boy
home. I cooked us all dinner. We shut the blinds.

Half Mexican

Whenever I start writing about identity I start doubting why I matter.

My husband was stopped on his way home from work. He was wearing his maroon nursing scrubs and hospital badge. The officer said he *fit a description*, held him on the side of the road for hours, called the nursing home where he dresses wounds to check his story. They were looking for a thug.

There's always something that matters more than what I'm doing.

I'm not compiling a list of microaggressions. I'm not even telling you my story.

*

Identity is slippery. My husband says what if people think I'm not *valid*, not really Latin@ because I'm half white. He's half black. He can say things like this. Or he's trying to make a point, playing devil's advocate. His words ricochet in my mind all week. I light candles at the altar I've made above my bed, in the window facing the Sandia Mountains, Spanish for watermelon, their pink glow at sunset. The candles drip wax down my wall, red-orange smudging whitewash, that stark paint.

Earlier in the day he took a sage smudge stick and burned it across our doorways, our walls.

I didn't choke on the smoke.

*

I explain to my white father why being Latin@ matters to me.

He's not arguing with me, sitting on the couch with a bag of Cocoa Puffs he's eating by the handful like chips or peanuts, a golf tournament on television. He's listening, crunch crunch, as I expound identity theory and erasure of the artist, crunch crunch, how *the author is dead* was born as women and minorities began publishing what they'd been hiding in closets, crunch crunch. He doesn't get it, but he's listening.

There was a time he and his dad used to say racist shit about Tiger Woods.

They've changed since I married my husband. They didn't just stop repeating the jokes, I mean, they even stopped thinking they were funny.

*

I share ancestry with Frida Kahlo: half Mexican half German. In fifth grade I took Mama's razor and shaved my legs, dry. I didn't know about soap and water, so I have a scar down my left shin. Mama told me she would've helped me if I'd told her why—my armpits too, my arms, my eyebrows. I plucked them into thatched rooftops, stark angles above my dark eyes.

Now I have nine Fridas on my walls, not including the doll Avra made me. None of them smile.

*

My dad drove a beige jalopy, picked me up from Sacred Heart every afternoon. The rich white kids laughed. They were *all* rich, the white kids. Children of farmers in our border town. We were there on scholarship.

My brother is full Mexican. I don't know if he feels different than I do or not. I've never asked him.

He grew up with our father too. But our father called him things like *your kid*, meaning Mama's, and *sissy boy* or *fag*. I hated our father too sometimes, when he said those things.

When my brother came out to his own father, on a fishing trip, when they were both grownups, his dad hugged him, said he loved him as boat lapped ocean. I wasn't there. I'm imagining the details.

*

We watched musicals every weekend, mama, my brother, and I.
Seven Brides for Seven Brothers, Hello Dolly, The Unsinkable Molly Brown,

Singing in the Rain, Oklahoma, Carousel. We sang all the songs.

*

I don't know if I can say that the Mexican kids never accepted me because I didn't speak Spanish. The white ones never understood our arroz con pollo, fighting for the burnt at the bottom of the pot, our tres leches and tortillas instead of bread. But that's a lie. They liked our food. They'd order it from Nana Dora's, their stay-at-home moms would deliver it to them at lunchtime. I ate cafeteria food.

When I was eleven the white kids dared me to eat a whole jalapeño; since I was Mexican, they said, it wouldn't sting.

My mom is full Mexican. She doesn't eat chile or jalapeños or salsa because of her ulcer.

Also, she has nothing to prove.

*

I'm not ashamed of my white father. Not anymore. I was never ashamed of him for being white.

Maybe for being poor. For wearing nothing but underwear when he got up in the mornings and went into the kitchen for his instant Folgers coffee crystals, or nothing but shorts (no shirt) when he was watering the front yard, baring his gleaming pale and hairy chest.

But I never much noticed he was white.

Not even at the dinner table when mama or abuela or anyone else would talk about those loco gringos.

*

Ice rain. Sleet. There was frozen water pouring all night into early morning when the police came to our door.

The welcome mat slippery, there are things we've endured.

TONY GLOEGGLER

On the Seventh Day

When God is leaning back,
all full of himself, and resting
on his laurels, I get up early,
go to my desk and try to take
his place, fill a few blank pages,
create my own world. Maybe
Monk's "Bright Mississippi"
or Ahmad Jamal plays
in the background
as the characters doo-wop
and stutter weave, in
and out, between, the lines:
a twenty-one year old
autistic boy, learning
to be on his own, bites
his wrist and slams
his head on the floor
and still can't tell me why,
my mom calls and we hardly
ever have much to say
except a cousin I never met
died of cancer yesterday,
a day before his 30th birthday,
and she wants me to buy a card,
write a hundred dollar check
to help pay for the plot, and yes
my heart is still slowly healing
from this summer's surgery
and the load of loneliness
that has always surrounded me
feels heavier as I struggle
to imagine what a good day
could ever be like again.

And when I take a breath
step out of my head,
I read about one more
young black man, his hair
freshly braided, walking
down another unlit
stairway with his girlfriend
in Brooklyn's Pink Houses
as a rookie cop patrols
the hallway toward him,
his gun unholstered, and opens
a door. I want to go back
to my desk and pretend
I'm God so I can write
how the bullet whizzes
past, ricochets harmlessly
to the floor since God
chose to sit idly by, act
like he had little to do
with any of it, content to speak
through some Sunday morning
preacher about a better place,
that the lord never gives more
than his children can bear,
how we will one day understand
his master plan when just once
I want God to stand up, shine
beacons of the brightest light
and share the shame and blame
while the wide world cries
with its head in its hands.

RUTH GORING

America, if

If the girl behind me on the bus hadn't poured
an interminable argument into her phone.
If the halls and sidewalks hadn't been slick.
If my neighbor's test had not been positive.

If anyone had found sweet memories to share
at my ex-father-in-law's funeral: a tune
he whistled, his favorite macaroni.

It there had been rain in the west, and snow.
If we'd stopped talking about everyone's hair.
If instead someone had written music
that stopped the deportation buses.

If I had been able to collect the gravel
and rain of myself, the barbed wire.
If the year had been a wide meadow.

If the police had lit lanterns.
If the borders between our countries.

Sonia Greenfield

Alternate Facts

We never thought it could happen here—
the poisoned, the disappeared—

these tunnels a network of news channels—
server room, keyboards, screens aglow

on damp, earthen walls—the reporter
bludgeoned in her bed & found

by her daughter—see this passage here?
this is where we shuttle journalists

through to California—our cell towers
are disguised as olive trees, but drones

pick them off, so we rebuild—don't mind
these spiders: their venom is better

than state-sanctioned firing squads—
how we lost half our staff, their families—

& don't mind the darkness pressing
against you here in the underground—

it is the medium we move news through
now that the mobs have bought the machine—

if I'm not back by morning, I was caught
& tortured by order of decree—

our Great Leader wants us all dead—
you, your loved ones, & me.

Because I'm from His Island

I've known this real estate
mogul with hair on fire
contractor with ass in flames
barker of steel at hardhats
who leer and sneer and think
his car is two years' wages,
this part-time boatsman
playing King of Clubs
at the court of Bulkhead Beach.

Because I'm from his island
I've known a woman wrapped and smuggled
like a Cuban cigar in embargo days
chuted in her father's blazer pocket
for after the wedding and Cordon Bleu
while groomsmen lynch hip-hop.

I've known a woman who believes
she can sail with all brown leaves
on the sunset wind she hears
can only whip up danger.
Because she's from his island
she's known the darker fables
but believed the lighter ones.

Because I'm from his island
I've read the fairy tales back to front
while parking in a strip mall lot
until a speeding Audi took me out
en route to Starbuck's, the driver
with his Uzi compressor drawn
about to spray a gawking crowd
with Second Amendment solution.

Because I'm from his island
I've watched immigrants' grandsons
ride through town in useless pick-up trucks
screaming Old West lines at landscape
peons. The prairie's overrun
the Appalachians, but they don't shoot
because they're from his island
and can't be bothered to mow their lawns.
I've seen grown men lament the height of lawns.
I've seen grown men believe
that all the world's a lawn.

Because I'm from his island
home to the oldest commuter trains
I've watched men asphyxiate themselves
to keep from sharing rides with strangers
mortgage their wives for three-year leases.
I've seen fathers load manors and groves
into SUVs, while mothers publicize
their souls, then lose accounts
when the UPS pulled up.
Because I'm from his island
I've seen children neatly, gently
strung from pressure-treated crosses
with designer rope, called
bullies for singing indoors
while behind the grade school lunchroom
parents forced movements down throats.

Because I'm from his island
I've seen bankers murder dollar bills
not to pardon them,
then complain about the state
of county parks. I've understood,
because I'm from his island,
even the dogs know something's wrong.
I see them run with human beings
fleeing black-sack media drops
from the twenty-four-hour sky.

No one ventures darkness
or lets the children dance through booby traps
beyond the alarmed perimeter.
Meanwhile on his island
we've failed to disarm the cable box.

Because I'm from his island
I've heard "nigger," "raghead," and "fag"
used like pronouns, sometimes
not by off-duty football cooks.
I've seen ordinary people hide
these words in cupboards,
sprinkle their remarks instead
with a dash of "African American,"
"foreigner," or "gay." But just as many
have revised their recipes,
thrown all the old ingredients
in a landfill tagged for park land.

Because I'm from his island
I'll stroll in the park with neighbors,
pretend I'm hiding inside heads
with all their best intentions.

LUKE HANKINS

The Answer

On some sacred page all the answers lie curled
like embryos waiting to be born.
In the meantime I'm trying to understand the world.

Every second, hungry bullets are hurled,
seeking whom they may devour. Be warned.
(Where's that sacred page where all the answers lie curled?)

Out of love, Confederate flags are unfurled
on trucks roaring through our towns.
Or maybe I've misunderstood the world.

We've armed everyone and are assured
threats are neutralized on a balanced battleground.
(In which ammo case do the proper instructions lie curled?)

The handle of my gun is beautiful—filigreed and pearled.
(The other end doesn't need to be adorned
to be adored.) The answer to your question? It's curled
around the sacred bullet flying through the world.

DAVID HERNANDEZ

All-American

I'm this tiny, this statuesque, and everywhere
in between, and everywhere in between
bony and overweight, my shadow cannot hold
one shape in Omaha, in Tuscaloosa, in Aberdeen.
My skin is mocha brown, two shades darker
than taupe, your question is racist, nutmeg, beige,
I'm not offended by your question at all.
Penis or vagina? Yes and yes. Gay or straight?
Both boxes. Bi, not bi, who cares, stop
fixating on my sex life, Jesus never leveled
his eye to a bedroom's keyhole. I go to church
in Tempe, in Waco, the one with the exquisite
stained glass, the one with a white spire
like the tip of a Klansman's hood. Churches
creep me out, I never step inside one,
never utter hymns, Sundays I hide my flesh
with camouflage and hunt. I don't hunt
but wish every deer wore a bulletproof vest
and fired back. It's cinnamon, my skin,
it's more sandstone than any color I know.
I voted for Obama, McCain, Nader, I was too
apathetic to vote, too lazy to walk one block,
two blocks to the voting booth. For or against
a woman's right to choose? Yes, for and against.
For waterboarding, for strapping detainees
with snorkels and diving masks. Against burning
fossil fuels, let's punish all those smokestacks
for eating the ozone, bring the wrecking balls,
but build more smokestacks, we need jobs
here in Harrisburg, here in Kalamazoo. Against
gun control, for cotton bullets, for constructing
a better fence along the border, let's raise
concrete toward the sky, why does it need
all that space to begin with? For creating
holes in the fence, adding ladders, they're not

here to steal work from us, no one dreams
of crab walking for hours across a lettuce field
so someone could order the Caesar salad.
No one dreams of sliding a squeegee down
the cloud-mirrored windows of a high-rise,
but some of us do it. Some of us sell flowers.
Some of us cut hair. Some of us carefully
steer a mower around the cemetery grounds.
Some of us paint houses. Some of us monitor
the power grid. Some of us ring you up
while some of us crisscross a parking lot
to gather the shopping carts into one long,
rolling, clamorous and glittering backbone.

These Are Brave Days

This is fucked this is not normal this is America
unzipping a garment bag then casually
sliding out the satin white floor-length robe
this is crazy witnessing our country slip
it on then the pointed hood this is foul
this is what we're going to do okay listen
call Speaker Ryan (202) 255-3031 and say
hello my name is then say your name
I'm calling from then say your city
then say there's been an uptick in whiskey
and Xanax since the President-elect
appointed a white nationalist to whisper
daily into his ear into his brain the same
landfill of racism they ram their snouts in
say Speaker Ryan say heart to heart say
these flames aren't putting themselves out
now stop gazing at that fire extinguisher
like it's some sculpture at MoMA
do something say something why aren't you
speaking Speaker Ryan speak for us Jesus
Christ cannonballing into a volcano
this is madness this is hurtful wow is this
how you want America to look at us
through eyeholes scissored into the hood
through us through our blood to spill it
and see were we came from I will tell you
it's the United Motherfucking States
then hang up and look out your window
and believe the fire is shuddering

LUTHER HUGHES

Not Splendor

November 8th
A television
A dagger of a name. A reason for weeping. A night of whiskey shots
at a bar pregnant with white. A phone call from family. Another
reason. A message about country. A phone call from brown. A little
dry eye. A sleep worth sleeping.

November 9th
A television
A morning splashed of orange.
A disgust, a peel from home. A walk in the dirty yellow, the smell
of green. Beat against the chest. Something in the sky, always. Bird
without wings. A blue snapped in half by memory. Suppose reason.
The meaning of wickedness as trophy.
The first step in cleaning the body is to recognize it.

A thigh
The boy I poured myself into, I can't stop. What a brown honey.
Skin is healing. Lips are certain about themselves. That's probably
true. Pink where it matters. Pink in the flower. Pink in the brain,
knotted.

A line
Stressed, unstressed stressedunstressed unstressed unstressed
stressed unstressed unstressed stressedunstressed unstressed
stressed stressedunstressed unstressed unstressed.

A tear
There is a man in a boat in a forked stream between expressions.
There is an expression that says things and choose which to inhale.
There is breath in the skin of skins. There is skin too far away to
hold. There is holding on to nothing. There is nothing but. There
is *but* which means instead of. There is *instead* between the cracks
of language. There is language for everything. There is everything
black and back and pull from. There is from the night moon.
There is the moon. There might by mourning.

November 10ᵗʰ
Another day
Another day.

November 11ᵗʰ
A blanket
A gray fieldwork, gray stitch work, gray comfort. A cotton overturned, over.
A time of remembrance. It's someone's deathday.
A pathway of lines etched in my hands. An extra hand is easy to come by.
CC: slavery.

A phone call from my mother
Someone from church has died.
It's my grandmother's birthday.

November 12ᵗʰ
A book about death
I hope nothing familiar braids my eyes closed.
How specific. The metaphor.
A mother says her son. I hope it ends the way it started. I hope a mother
angel. Come say this is for what it's worth. Come say dog-ear the page
without saying dog-ear the page.
Relax is only a verb. What else relaxes splays the dead. I do. I do and the
moon slips. Stupid moon. See, "earth."

A Jack'd message
Them lips 😍
Hey whats up
?
Hey
Hey
Wyd
Fuck you nigger

A plate of fried chicken
Where God birthed light with voice, a moment of silence. A sign of bloom.
The resemblance: little blackbird in the mirror. What of Trayvon?
This is a shape about color. Fried is not black. Black is not black. What is
black but a diamond from the ground. That's not a real question. I have
five of them. The first one is the juiciest.

A response from me
hey.

November 13th
A robin
Dead and chestless in the alley. Come maggots, croon maggots, sleep maggots. Where red lingers, my eyes. I rope my fingers inside my pockets, pull out a feather. Metaphor happens here and the feather is white.

A robin
A night veil slithers into my mouth and my mouth black as hell and hell is a bird and a bird is a heart and a heart is a nightmare and a nightmare is a cold shower and a cold shower is a memory and a memory is weeping.

A crane in the sky
The room swallows Solange's voice and what's vacant trembles: ocean of sorrow. I think of home, a harbor of things I swore to escape: an interiority of doubt. The song hues everything my eyes digest. How unlikely a crane bled by beats—and my tears have tiny flies.

November 14th
A plastic water bottle
Cue the war on everything: a forest fabricated into the body and the body slapped dangerous.

November 15th
A remote control
Somewhere is a city of graveyards sunk beneath forgetfulness. Somewhere a fist pummels into a wall named Anger. What lays inside the finger's curl leaves the dead an empty valley. What misses blood. The dirt creates a relationship and a child wants to know what happened to his father.
Here's the channel about change.
I should switch.
I have a glass of wine that spills on my black shirt.

A crane in the sky
On the couch in the living room, a hunger red in the belly. What deserves: the sound of water thrashing in the fallen water bottle, the *Fresh Prince of Bel-Air* theme song under a hum, a text message that says "Hey stranger."

A Vote Trump sticker
Beetles parade for their anniversary of life within the earth-black moisture.
This is what nature intended as end: a pasture of insects feeding on grief.

November 16ᵗʰ
A Vote Trump sticker
As if pain were a shirt, the body slips into. Pain is sometimes untraceable,
gathering in the lowest pocket. I pray to a God with no eyesight, carve
myself limp. Just below the surface are bones, but useless. What stops
tragedy has no place in the body. We are always failing.
A sky bent over. An earth left to wither. Spell it out: the moment of *fuck*.
How many days does it take for feeling to staple? I have hands and a
nervous system. Sometimes I react to things I never touched.

A boy
I touch the flesh-rod with my tongue. I swoop him into my mouth like a
bowl. I father a moan. I sew my eyes. I swallow an ancestor.

A plate of fried chicken
It's always about race with this.

November 17ᵗʰ
A woman with a pink shirt
Nude is not the color of all.

November 18ᵗʰ
A Jack and Coke
I place you inside my mouth, want to forget everything. Another way to say
take me earth is to drown myself in the earth's liquor. Where does it come
from. I am the light in the empty glass. "Another." The ice cubes swallow
light, too. I am light, remember? Look at the men dance in the dark as the
dust rises to coffin them. I want a coffin like that: men.

A moon
Pretty lady with the white eye, how goes the weeping?

A ride home
The color of things rest beneath my skin: red, white, blue.
I wonder what the sun is doing right now. Is that weird? Probably so.

A bedroom
Messy mouth.

A glass of water
Messy mouth.

> *November 19ᵗʰ*
A painting
See, "*November 10ᵗʰ*."
> *November 20ᵗʰ*
A laugh
The cackle of the wind is another reason for sorrow. The cackle of the wind harvests the kitchen. The cackle of the wind stitches stillness. The cackle of the wind throws the trees into panic. The cackle of the wind swallows the cicadas. The cackle of the wind tosses my clothes. The cackle of the wind swells inside my mouth. The cackle of the wind loosens. The cackle of the wind births sorrow. The cackle of the wind sifts. The cackle of the wind unbraids its hair. The cackle of the wind lies down with fleas. The cackle of the wind guns the body crisp. The cackle of the wind follows.

A fruit cup
The grapes are soggy.

A phone call from my brother
He's laughing again. Good news.

A nap
The shadow has a head of owl feathers, blonde. When it swoops into my mouth, I name myself nest. I am pretty on all ends. The sticks and stones will supplement my bones. There is blood that creeps from one end to the next like a house rat.

A television
Memory of weeping.

> *November 21ˢᵗ*
A squirrel
Little scavenger, where is your family?

A classroom
Salt and pepper. More salt than pepper, though, can I really complain?

A television
The brown boy says "you're racist" to his best friend. The audience laughs. I am eating an orange.
My brother is here.

November 22nd
A brother
A kind of bird.

Self-Portrait as Crow

I.

I've always been a sucker for being eaten alive.

One eye, like a dark rose, drips from the fox's maw, spills
its beauty. Instead of "caw," it is *help* that adorns
my beak. As the petalled-eye hangs there, watches me
watch it unbloom into the fox's taste,

an old wave of blackness washes over me.

I've never been more menaced. Some of me stay
when the fox leaves, flees into the nearest greenery. I glitter
a slow stain to the buzz of the streetlight, its cross-hatch smile
across everything: *if only he'd stop resisting, the poor bird would still be alive.*

II.

My gore lingers into the next dawn. It is spring.

The season brings me a wooden casket to rest
my remains. I'm wrapped in traditional wear—earth tones
and yellow. Waiting. Flora broken beside me.
Before the sirens come, I summon a flock of savages

with my dead: a natural magic. But this is nothing new.

My brother and sisters raise their wings to the crowgods, I watch
the murder surround. Some sit at my limp, bow
heads of grief. Others remain a shadow hovering.
The silent ones cram pieces of anger into the muscles' wax.

Replace the protein. Fuel their rage.

KENAN INCE

Sickle

from the Proto-Indo-European sek, *meaning to cut, or to divide.*
See also schism, sex, science.

The first man who used it
to slice the stalks of wheat
was not a shaman,
but when he swung the blade
did he feel the tear
in possibility?
Did he taste the blood
of the future that might have been?
Did he hear the howl
of machines from afar?
If so, did he think it
a swarm of bees? Was his vision
of dancing fire, and women
held by chains attached
to metal collars,
and people singing
strange songs full of regret
while they passed metal shards
down an assembly line?
Did he see the water
turn to blood, and the fish
of the river die,
and the water stink,
and the people loathe to drink
of the water? Did he wonder
what god had performed
such plagues? Could he have guessed?
Did it matter whether
it was man or God who led him
to harden his heart
and close his eyes
and let the sickle whine through the air?

Mollusks

In my fantasies, I'm always walking
downstairs in my sensible flats.
Something about them arouses me:
the way they can be so easily slipped
off, their black skeletons crumpling
in my closet until I am ready to give
them flesh. They are no animal.
They are as little as possible
between me and the caress
of the earth on my feet. Oh,
how Donald Trump would love
for me to take them off
and float through the halls
behind him like a caveman's
wife, hand on my swollen belly!
How Donald's mouth would swell
on the aerodynamic curved tip
as I inserted my foot, softly,
between his lips. How
he would suck as if to aspirate
out the vital part of me.
And how he would gasp, his lungs
collapsing into the garden
of his ribs, his words scurrying
before they are spoken
from the shell of his mouth.

Resolution*

Ten men with assault rifles
strapped to their chests
stand masked in the parking lot
across from the mosque.
One of them carries
a *Ted Cruz for Senate* sign
from 2010. In the picture,
there is no sense
of scale to the American flag
one of them carries:

it could be on a monument
a mile away and ten miles high
or a Fourth of July decoration
uprooted from a country lawn
forty minutes south on I-45,
to be waved on the first
cool day of the season
in Irving, Texas, of all places

I thought I'd never hear of
again, now that my Muslim dad
has moved to a richer, whiter
exurb. There is no sense
of scale: zoomed in, these angry men
could be soldiers raising the flag
in the fine North Texas sod
after some apocalyptic war,

reclaiming their country from boys
with ticking homemade weapons,
boys whose names sound
like they're gathering spit
in their mouths before striking,
like adders, so that you
have to kill them, in self-defense.
Like clockwork, these brown boys,
their faces intent, lips cocked
like AK-47s. Like the boy

at MacArthur High whose clock
could still be a bomb, ticking
in an evidence locker somewhere
waiting for us to forget. These boys
make a desert of your thoughts,
hot, immediate, and deadly.

These boys, twirling pencils
like dervishes, taking derivatives
in their heads, brown skin pressed
against your body, brown hands
raised to stuff your sure-thing layup
back into your arms, so they won't just
let you just be better than them
at something. You can't let them
take over your country
with their derka-derka,

as one protester spits to his AR-15-
draped friend, both of them
hurling laughter like rockets
at the dim November sun.
The Islam I was raised in
has always felt more distant
than these angry men,
always men, always white-

knuckled from clenching
too tight to the broken
machinery of privilege, always cranking
again and again the levers
of xenophobia, expecting
that next time health insurance
or a living wage will come out.

The Islam I learned exclusively
from tossed-off maxims about prayer
and "doing good" is nothing
to hold, nothing as hard

and metallic as the fact
of these rifles, barrels looming
closer to the brown bodies
of my family and friends,
to my own body which looks as white
as those of the men in bandanas
and fatigues and LL Bean jackets
who want to "examine" refugees

up-close, run their smooth tactical
shotguns over their brown bodies,
"see how many are actually
women and children."
Through the scope of the Islam
in which I was raised
the Texas red ants on the ground
loom as large as infants,
so as a child I held my legs
off the ground to avoid
becoming a murderer.

In the zoomed-out press
photos, the assault rifles
look as small as black ants.
"Nobody was listening to me
two or three weeks ago,"
a spokesman for the protesters
says, camera panning to reporters
around him, adding them
to the crowd. "Now look, now look,
now look how many people
are listening to me."

*All quotes from: "A weekend of angst over Islam: Guns in Richardson,
marchers in Dallas and a quiet conversation in Irving,"
The Dallas Morning News, December 15, 2015

Trickle-Down Theory

Here in Texas when we turn on
    the water the oil creeps through
        the hose into our cars' waiting tanks.
      Our showers are always hot and thick
        and our skin glistens for days.
                    Molly next door drinks a bottle
           straight. Our morning coffee
              pours slow but powers us for days.

How can you say we're running
        out of fuel when the oil rains
            from the skies? It coats our crops
       with its thick black milk. Here in Texas
    we've prayed for rain so long
    we dance in the streets
    when the black downpour starts.
              Our congressmen write bills
               to praise Valero and Exxon.

          I think we asked for it, these
forty days of rain. We asked for it
      for not having a summer
   house to pack up for when
       the floods come. Or for being born
          on the wrong side of the levees.
  When they open and the water
      beads together in the widening
                  crack, we think we've never seen
anything more beautiful. And we think
             maybe this is what we need,
  a clean slate. It's almost refreshing,
        like the first wellings
    of pride as fireworks explode
         over our kids' heads. "It's
like a theme park forever,"
      we tell them when they ask
about heaven. "Like Hawaii.
        Never drops below sixty."

We'll sit
     at the beach all day and watch the Earth below
                 as an invisible hand distills
        away the impure until
             all that is left of humanity
  is our constituent
     carbon. It is all
      we will ever give
        back to the world. It is all
        the generosity we contain.

Ode to United Fruit

Rainbows of mangos, bananas, and guavas line boxes in a warehouse, baking under equatorial sun. Good that someone knows how to transmute the raw materials of life into such goodwill packages, dripping with seeds like cluster bombs. Good that someone can gather coconuts lying like trained militias on Cuban shores and stack them into formation. What nature needs is order. Break down the borders that divide us from Guatemala, the Dominican Republic, Honduras, with boatloads of pineapples and tamarinds! No one will ever ask for their papers despite their brown skin: we remove the skin of a thing before we consume it. Plantain, *mamey sapote*, papaya: our dream of a unified race. Tones averaged to a blushing orange; virginal bride on her wedding night. *Nopal, tomatillo, chayote* squash: wait until ripe to invade with mouth or serving fork. *Manioc*, Adam's fig, *fruta bomba* straining to drop from the branch: please don't fall before we're ready.

MARIA MELENDEZ KELSON

El Villain

"I fled the West Coast to escape them, but I still see illegals
Everywhere," whines a letter-writer in our rural Utah paper,
Applauding a local ICE raid. "How does it feel to be a problem?"

Everyone (no one) wanted to ask Du Bois, circulating his elegant
Diction and mixed-race face among Atlanta glitterati, turn
Of the century, when the White Sixth Sense was "I can smell

Negroes and Jews." The question ices my hair and eyelashes,
All Raza one family of suspects in this age of round-ups; am I
To breathe in prejudice, breathe out light? How does it feel

To be a problem? Some well-meaning White ones want a Christ of
Me, sacred heart on display. "Where are your documents
Naming this pain?" They hope for a nibble of rage. I see Lourdes,

Seven years old and *sin documentos,* embrace my daughter hello,
Good-bye, every day on their school's front steps, the two of them
Giddy with girl pacts. When Lourdes solves subtraction problems,

Safe at her dim kitchen table, how does her mother, Elva, feel,
As her daughter works a language that will never add up to home?
Down the street, I see Rodolfo from El Salvador, legal refugee, dance

The glee of a Jazz victory in front of his big screen. Ask him how
Pupusas feel in his mouth, corn-dough communion with *patria.* His wife,
Inez, is fourth-generation Mexican American from Salt Lake City.
                    Fuck these pedigrees. How does it feel

For Rodolfo, Inez, Lourdes, me, to be seen as not-quite-right,
Not quite US, not from around here, are ya?
I will not say. I will not display our stigmata.

We shouldn't need papers to cross from familia to politics.
Ask the seer-of-illegals, the maid of ethnic cleansing,
How it feels to hold a broken feather duster.

RUTH ELLEN KOCHER

Skit: Sun Ra Welcomes the Fallen

Jupiter means anger. Sun Ra does not. Sun Ra dances the Cake Walk on Saturn's pulpy eyes. If you believe that, I'll tell you another one. The first is 13 and the next is 20. They were not good boys but they were boys. They were boys who died for this thing or that. The next was 16 and the last was 18. One had a cell phone. One had a gun. On earth, a goose opens its chest to a sound. The goose takes the bullet this way. A sacrifice denied to the wind since there is no such thing as sacrifice anymore having succumbed to fever and the millennium. The bullet is all consequence. Sun Ra refuses red—long and high, low and deep. His arms are long enough to embrace them.

DANA LEVIN

Winning

When you meet need,
beat it blind with a baseball bat,
beat it and beat it—
because loss means
    (duh)
that you are a loser.

Don't wash your face
in the bowl
of your empty hands, don't
count the days
you've soaked in its pit
finger by finger.

If you lose you have to
lose more. That's
the natural order.

You need to wear a pair
of black boots,
a T-shirt
slashed with the word
    —WINNER—
So when you meet a loser

you can offer him
your charity. Lift your bat
above his misery

and win and win and win.

TIMOTHY LIU

Protest Song

Do I have to
comfort you,

little ones?

The cancer
has spread

deep into

the country,
even beyond

the outlying

provinces.
The Christian

god won't bring

back coal.
And don't you

think the air

is too full of it
already? You

can't fight

the lower
wages across

the border,

and besides
this will mean

others will

have more
reasons to stay

on their own

side where we
know they

have always

belonged. Fear
not. This

is how we make

America great
again as, one

by one, million

dollar mansions
crumble into

an unforgiving

sea, not one
then, but two

Americas

as the borders
that have

been drawn

start to redraw
themselves

again, can't

you smell
the fear inside

their blood

just before
it's shed?

The pipeline

will not
go through,

not if

any of us
can help it.

Goddamn

the buffalo
gathered on

the horizon

if they aren't
ready to

stampede

for they know
which side

we're taking,

water cannon
fire be

damned,

concussion
grenades

be damned—

lobbed across
lands we hold

most sacred.

A man without
a soul-friend

is like a lake

no good
for bathing

nor drinking

so fear not,
little ones,

the ancestors

won't leave us
the same way

shit jobs

have already
left them

holding on

to nothing
more than

a tiny

scorched
tract of earth

called home.

DENISE LOW

Andrew Jackson, I See You

I spindle, wad, and trade you for tens,
but banks dispense more of your face—
flaring hair, horsey face, sharp cheeks,
arrogant look of moral rightness.

I see an outlaw who betrayed Creeks,
double-crossed the Supreme Court,
seized Cherokee farms and gold mines,
and ordered many Trails of Tears.

Today, your bills are common trash.
Americans everywhere squash you,
squat walleted butt-cheeks over you,
cram you into purses with tissue.

Cell phones clang in your big ears,
bartenders spill whiskey up your nose,
sloppy eaters smear you with fries,
kids deface you with ink disguises.

New Orleans nuns saved you for this
afterlife of paper zombie confetti.
Users roll you and snort dope. Still,
Andy, this hell is far too good.

GEORGE ELLA LYON

This Just In from Rancho Politico

We the haves
have nots
we the cranked up
bankrupt
money wells
splinter cells
ne'er do wells
who can tells
We the peep-hole!

We the peep-hole
We the emails
hemails
shemails
camp pain trails
gotta gitmo jails
off the rails

know it all
border wall
recompense
poison fence
red phone
not my home

FYI
apple pie
DIY
tell me why
Trumpus rumpus
trying to humpus

Sea rise
cyber spies
Flint water
future slaughter

Blessed are the rich
who incentivize the poor
ban immigration
bolt that golden door

Peep-Hole, pay attention!

We the Peep-Hole
of the Untied Hates of America
      (Ferguson
      another son
      Michael Brown
      gunned down
      Script is set
      that's what you get
      for going around being
      black)
in ordure to form
a more profitable Corporation
concealed in Liberty
and dedicated to the propped position
that all money is created equal

Will you vote for that?

Or sit on the bleak cheers waiting to see
how it all falls out?

NO, Peep-Hole!
This is our rodeo!
We gotta put on our boots—
those big shit-stompers—
and saddle up for the chute.

You gotta rope 'em and ride 'em
at Rancho Politico.
Gotta hold your nose and vote!

J. Michael Martinez

The Mexican War Photo Postcard Company

On March 9th, 1916 General Francisco "Pancho" Villa raided the village of Columbus, New Mexico. Soldiers of the 13th US Calvary & nine townspeople were executed while the town itself was pillaged & burned.

A few days after, Walter H. Horne of The Mexican War Photo Postcard Company documented a village possessed by ruin: the images are a phantasmagoria of smoldering ash blacked stone, of smoke curdling above dead Villista raiders in their cremation pit, and the dilated eyes of roan stallions.

Employing an inexpensive emulsion known as "gaslight," Horne was able to successfully print tens of thousands of postcards. Selling up to 5,000 "real-photo" postcards a day to U.S. soldiers during the Mexican Revolution, Horne was responsible for a vast photographic immigration of nameless Mexicans desired only as epistles anchored in their death.

"Triple Execution in Mexico"
A Postcard Set by William H. Horne

i.

White frames the sepia

      & six rifles raise
      as gateways respiring

linguistic traces;

ever of his death, the executed
shuffles over exodus

      as if dancing:

fingers cawed in black, chin

obscure against the tumor'd

pearls of smoke,   body as text now one

of those things the shadow outlines
on which is built another chariot.

ii.

Unnailed in cross,   the second
leans forward into crucifixion

arms upstretched as wingbones
wrought of tar. Quickened as postcard,

he would be drowned
in sodium carbonate:

brown bowl haircut & coveralls,
grimacing & eyes pitched

in clouds of silver halide.
Smoke rises in minor triumph

behind him as if the soul
were the emulsion

evading the image.
Lined as background stick figures,

a crowd of children gathers dust
& shade beside the spectacle:

if there are tears, there are no homilies;
if there is color, they are bronze;

if there is life, it is public domain;
if he had a name, it is now transnational

confusion
postmarked in relief.

iii.

Face a soft blur beneath his hair, the boy leans stiffly as if posing
against the palisade. Hide boots are scuffed grey with dirt. A book
peeks up from his jacket pocket. The words weigh the pocket down.
He leans. A young riot, his hair parts into a black gorge against his
cheek. Handwritten, he is titled, "Triple Execution in Mexico #3."
Handwritten, the book peeks forward as if to part from his falling.
His hand raises as if for an offered kiss. The left hand loses a coin.
The coin falls into his title. The title is drawn where even shape
hesitates. To his left, the two words he will join stare thru the paper
sky.

"Execution in Mexico"

A Postcard by William H. Horne

Composed for the golden ratio, the boys hang from the mesquite. They know nothing of adolescence. Facing each other, their bodies blur into landscape—the older boy's head rests to the side as if listening for a whisper; noose taut, his left hand raises, cradling a brighter spill to his chest. The younger boy's chin is lost up in leaf shadow, rope crushing his neck to the branch.

However, they are shoeless &, to the far right, three men in linen suits fade white as smiles into the background.

They are shoeless &, above them, the branches tangle for a crown of bronze light ever arriving & still.

Perpetually of this acetate death, they are always in each other's hand.

"Yncineracion de Cadaveres en Balbuena"
Postcard No 35

The mound of piled cadavers
splays in clots of coal
coated skin;

faces clamor
& throb as one

hundred arms, stiff as a singed tin
soldiers,

reach across this drowning
as if casting their names
between the surface & depth

of the postcard's visual space.
Nearly lost to the border,

an iron bed
frame, weighted black   by crumbling mouths,
performs its last purpose in solitude.

&, centered below their title, smoke rises

like a flag from the ragged

clothing   burnt to calcium

white: violence seizing

the emblem   as flesh
collapses through fact.

"Executing Bandits in Mexico"
A Postcard by William H. Horne

Blindfolded before the creosote,
the man waits. Out of the pale,

embodied thru copper contrast,

the executioners anchor the foreground:
six rifles raise toward the subject

line, cacti faint against the border.

The man's arms are
amputated by luminance,

as his boots crush the grey pickleweed.

A single tentacle sky
blanches the background,

absence throttling
the aperture light.

The Executioner's Palisade

A Postcard by William H. Horne

One wall binds
death to death,

a partition of skin,
adrenalin & hair.

Adobe
& mesquite

pull bodies without flesh northward,
migrant anatomy ever unlocked

as the otherside of language.
Stamped for address,

the paper carcass seals
word to image,
postscript to passage;

the Mexican—all virgin talisman
when mailed in a sepia ruin

whose only wound is postage—
the distance the body travels
to know another.

Yet, they, dark gardens, swing exhausted,
every organ a throne,

rebroken & rewritten
into simpler stems, leaves, & seeds,

body laid between

what only flesh can mediate
while flesh.

SHANE McCRAE

Everything I Know About Blackness I Learned from Donald Trump

> "Frederick Douglass is an example of somebody who's done an amazing
> job and is being recognized more and more, I notice."
> —Donald Trump

America I was driving when I heard you
Had died I swerved into a ditch and wept
In the dream I dreamed unconscious in the ditch
America   I dreamed you climbed from the ditch
You must believe your body is and any
Body and stood beside the ditch for eight years
Thinking   except you didn't stand you right
Away lay down on your pale belly
And tried to claw your way back to the ditch
You right away began to wail   and weep
And gnash your teeth   my tears met yours in the ditch
America   they carry me downstream
A slave on the run from you   an Egyptian queen
Even in my dreams I'm in your dreams

Sjohnna McCray

Portrait of My Father as a Young Black Man
Cincinnati, Ohio, 1987

Rage is the language of men,
    layers of particulates fused.

    Rage is the wine
        father pours to the ground

        for men whose time has passed. Rage
        is gripped in the hands

    like the neck of a broom held tight. Rage
gets stuck in the throat, suppressed.

Rage is a promise kept.

Burning Down Suburbia

an Ode to Bob Ross

When I was younger, I watched the world blend
    on PBS. The painter with the *Jewfro* hypnotized me.

With a thumb hooked through the palette,
    he painted forward from the base coat

like a god might use a blueprint.
    Behind the image is always the word:

light. On top came tiny crisscross strokes
    of phthalo blue. A rapturous pinwheel of words

unveiled sky. Two sharp strokes of titanium white
    slashed with gray from the master's knife

became wings, gulls taking flight. I begged for nothing
    but paints that summer. Already equipped with an afro,

I sat before the paper and the cakes of color
    and tried to figure out the path to cerulean,

the wrist twist to evergreens and the motion
    for clouds. The oversaturated paper dried and cracked

with the fine lines of lightning. The worlds he reproduced
    might as well have been Asgard or Olympus.

How I longed for a visit. Might he come
    armed with a fan brush and dressed in a button down?

To be soothed by his voice and taken,
    lured from the dining-room table and shown

the suburb's majesty. Look son, he might say,
    at the pile of autumn leaves, the shade

on that forest-green trash bag. Using his two-inch brush
    he'd blend the prefab homes on the hill

until they seemed mysterious, folded hues
    of Prussian blue, Van Dyke brown, and a blaze of alizarin crimson.

Price Check

At the A&P, angry men with matted hair
         and fistfuls of change drop their coins

in front of the register. They pile cans
         of potted meat on the belt and reluctantly wait

as the cashier shuffle-counts pennies
         into the palms of his hand. *Stupid college boy.*

There's a shelter next door that leans to the right
         like a drunk with cracked white shutters

and spray-painted columns tagged with gang signs.
         An apocalyptic Tara in the heart of Midtown.

The smell of the patrons lingers all day:
         KOOLs, sex and damp T-shirts. A woman with too much rouge

digs through an old purse. Her wig is slanted
         and she needs two dimes. Or four nickels.

A Victorian gone awry. Something about the intensity,
         the absolute belief that two small coins

will appear, reminds the cashier of his mother—
         the day the odd car pulled up to the lawn.

He's seven and she's been gone for months.
         She's freshly scrubbed and her face is blanched.

His father tips the driver and his mother
         searches a small, clear bag with a comb, Vaseline,

and countless tin wrappers folded like birds
         for one stick of gum. She hands it to him

like it's her only possession and he counts it
         as if it's all that he needs.

ERIKA MEITNER

I'll Remember You as You Were, Not as What You'll Become

If you are fearful, America,
I can tell you I am too. I worry
about my body—the way, lately,
it marches itself over curbs and
barriers, lingers in the streets
as a form of resistance.

The streets belong to no one
and everyone and are a guide
for motion, but we are so numerous
there is no pavement left on which to
release our bodies, like a river spilling
over a dam, so instead my body
thrums next to yours in place.

When we stop traffic or hold
hands to form a human chain,
we become a neon OPEN sign
singing into the night miles from
home when the only home left
is memory, your body, my body,
our scars, the dark punctuated
with the dying light of stars.

note: the title comes from the work of video artist Sky Hopinka

RAJIV MOHABIR

Inaugural Poem

Orange clouds warn: worry
will break down the door.

What happens below their cover
reflects against their bellies.

Another night I tithe
coins like hope for my
lady of sorrow. I phone

my mother so someone will hear
her prayers in Florida.

    —Ma?

She left London after
the National Front chased her

like a fox, immigrant and brown-
skinned. Today hounds
release hell along the roads,

those hiding in the underbrush
scatter. White boys beat

a Saudi student to death
in Menomonie. Klansmen
with hats like teeth march

the streets in North Carolina—

    Ma are you there? Call me back
    let me know you are still alive.

On the walls of my high school
some white hands scrawl
"better start picking yall slave numbers KKK"

    Ma, this is only miles from you.

In Oviedo, twenty miles
from Sanford, Christians claim
this an exception.

Even in Honolulu a student scribbles
"black lives have never mattered."

I look around and think that two
out of every three white Christians

want me dead. We all know
exactly how this happened.

    Yes, Ma, I'm okay.

Yet, in the north a buffalo stamps
the head of a snake, three black women
start and continue a movement,

and I have been smashing
all of the walls I can see until,
finally, my own walls collapse

and a hibiscus trumpets its pollen,
a bee holds its seed and carries
grains into the next bloom,

a movement cradles a community
after a white man opens fire in a church.

    Ma, they died mid-prayer.

A wildfire rages from a spark
of flowers, to glow daffodil,
rose, hibiscus, lehua,

> *Ma, I was wrong.*
> *Against the clouds what first*
> *I thought doom will mean*
> *our petals will not be plucked,*
> *how with America's hate*
> *our resistance grows, how*
> *under cement, roots break*
> *hate's fake stones,*
> *despite so much weight.*

FAISAL MOHYUDDIN

Song of Myself as a Tomorrow

> "It is not far—it is within reach;
> Perhaps you have been on it since you were born, and did not know;
> Perhaps it is everywhere, on water and on land."
> —Walt Whitman

In America—where my face is anything
but American, I lunge for self-annihilation whenever
another set of monstering eyes double-barrels me

                                        enemy
    outsider
                sandnigger
                                      terrorist
murderer   thief
            target practice
                      less-than
        dog   shitface   trespasser
                      imposter
   invader
            camel jockey
                    terrorist   *Muslim*
abuser
        enemy   foreigner
                    disembodied
             Bedouin

But erasure—
            what can it do when the blood's trajectory
has forever been about becoming another river, about winding its way
along some other pathway toward survival? How else
could I have come to be when
                pillage
                                  loss
       civil war   Partition
            loss
  displacement   Partition   loss

                                        silence
        Partition   loss
                                   migration   heartache
  grief   separation   loss
                                        displacement
        Partition
                              displacement   silence
        migration   loss
                                   Partition
        Partition

                                        displacement
                              silence
                              hunger

                    touched every moment
                    of my parents' lives
                    cobbled together

                    onto the unlived tomorrows of children?
                    To plunge into tomorrow requires the existence
                    of a tomorrow to plunge into—

  I am that tomorrow, lost within the land
  beyond where all rivers end,
  in the barren vastness of an untethered
  darkness where survival means

  remembering my parents' tomorrows,
  knifing new furrows through which their refugee blood
  can flow—
  means saying, despite the price
  of standing tall and free,
                              Yes
                                                      to exile
                              Yes

        to America

KAMILAH AISHA MOON

Notes on a Mass Stranding

I.

Huge dashes in the sand, two or three
times a year they swim like words
in a sentence toward the period
of the beach, lured into sunning
themselves like humans do—
forgetting gravity,
smothered in the absence
of waves and high tides.

II.

[Pilot whales beach themselves] when their sonar
becomes scrambled in shallow water
or when a sick member of the pod
heads for shore and others follow

III.

61 of them on top of the South Island
wade into Farewell Spit.
18 needed help with their demises
this time, the sharp mercy
of knives still the slow motion heft
of each ocean heart.

IV.

Yes—even those born pilots,
those who have grown large and graceful
lose their way, found on their sides
season after season.
Is it more natural to care
or not to care?

Terrifying to be reminded a fluke
can fling anything or anyone
out of this world.

V.

Oh, the endings we swim toward
without thinking!
Mysteries of mass wrong turns, sick leaders
and sirens forever sexy
land or sea.
The unequaled rush
and horror of forgetting
ourselves.

A Superwoman Chooses Another Way to Fly

woke up again parched from a dream
full of old water, the only urgent tide
in me lately. eddies of sweat,
promise perishing in each exhale.

i matter too why didn't i believe i matter
more than an unblinking, shadowed eye
that refused to look at me with love?

perched on the edge of a day
that could be owl or ostrich—
wise flight or kicking dust,
i pray for wings that sprout beyond
my body if i must be
out of proportion, that my angers
rinse away into the drain
and i'm not driven mad by small
crawlings all over and through me,
by what has branded me
for the rest of this life.

it's always a choice, the angel spoke-sang,
to be stronger than what pulls
us down. let these night sweats
rain a salty hope, despite waking up
full of old water with the flaked mouth
of a sharecropper at dusk.
why settle for shacks when i own
a sprawling, rambling heart?
why stay thirsty when
many draw from my well?

in the bushes, a cat wails
like a woman forced
to defend something precious.
i toss my crumpled sheet
like a discarded cape
and rise, shoulder blades
aching to split open and bloom

What James Craig Anderson's Ghost Might Say (July 26, 2011)

> "How can this be? How can more than half a dozen teenagers take
> part in such a fatal racist attack in a region and a nation with a
> history of racial violence and most of them just be allowed to walk
> away from it? [...] Welcome to 21st century Mississippi."
> —Michael Deibert, *Huffington Post*

As young white fists and feet
fueled by heirloom fury landed
soundly into my flesh

and later, when the green
Ford F250 roared like fans
at a football game and I
staggered, 49 and bruised,
into bright
glassy eyes, I only thought

of my poor tax-paying,
church-going mother
who had the audacity to believe
with every chamber
of her Jackson-bred (not Jasper, TX)
heart, that the rise of Obama
meant no more Evers or Tills—
until they called her
to peel me
from Mississippi concrete.

Abby E. Murray

A Story for Our Daughters
Wednesday, November 9, 2016

When God saw
what he'd done,
the cancerous rib
in one hand,
his sleeping child
in the other,
he shaped us
from the squash
plant instead, braiding
vines and gold
blossoms into bones.
Then he made
us dream survival
was the only
gift he had
left to give.
All else was
claimed or taken,
he wasn't clear,
still manic, dazed.
Then we woke,
my dear daughter,
all of us
in a borrowed
world, the salt
and rock and
spine of it.
The sky boiled
with comets building
someone else's light.
Our partner was
terrified. He chattered
in the dirt
while we ran

our hands over
everything, my daughter,
thorns, teeth, words,
none of it
ours, the embers
and splinters, shards
of spilt creation.
The blood moved
through our hearts
like soldiers stamping
through a tunnel.
Nothing could kill
us, not even
love, not us.
This is it,
my daughter, survival
given to us
like territory, like
borders, like dust.

Poem for My Daughter Before the March

When your father says
he doesn't want me to march
what he really means is
he doesn't want you to march.

He doesn't want me to march
because you will follow.
He doesn't want you to march
by default, on my shoulders,

because you might follow
the songs of women
by default, on my shoulders,
raised on bread and justice.

Daughter, the songs of women
are the first words of children
raised on bread and justice.
Blessed are the ones who sing

the first words of children:
this is how I love you.
Blessed are the ones who say
they follow songs into the street.

My Daughter Asked for This

It is too late for sleep,
too early for rising
when I buy my daughter's
first Barbie,
my laptop at 5% as I squint
into the cow eyes
of a woman who bends
at the hips and shoulders
but cannot open her jaw
or make a fist.
My daughter asked for this.
She arrives without clothes,
she is what Mattel calls
sun-sational, a handful of daisies
creeping up the front
of her painted swimsuit.
My throat closes like a church,
which is to say it opens for air
and latches itself
against knowing better.
Dear baby angels of the blue hour
please let me buy this doll
and wrap it obediently
in butcher paper,
place it under our dying tree
like a sacrifice. Let me
write my daughter's name
on the reindeer tag
and not the warnings I wish
I'd had: beware the hands
that never punch
and the tiptoe feet
too arched for sprinting.
Hey, younger me, beware
how close the sky seems,
it is further than your father knew.
The Barbie is as good as bought
and in my defeat
I buy her an outfit too,

a $22 spacesuit complete
with gauzy leggings
and puffy boots.
The pink helmet
looks promising.
Every Christmas, I wish
I had a way to breathe
on worlds where I am
not quite home,
not quite a guest.

SUSAN NGUYEN

Good Girls

Our family vacations involved renting
a 15-seater minivan and driving x hours
north to Canada or x hours south to Florida.
The white van looked like the one I imagined
bad men used to lure children—behind those
doors would be Red Vines and Snickers and hands
ready to abscond with your body leaving you
dead in the roots of a swamp, strangling
you with your own pantyhose. The papers told
me they didn't care how old you were and my mother
taught me Good Girls always wear pantyhose.
We fought about it often. I hated the way the itchy
nylon was always falling, extra fabric gathering
in rolls. I imagined my skin melting, thought
of the black-and-white photo I'd seen of the nine-
year-old Napalm Girl running in the streets
of Vietnam, her skin on fire. I didn't feel bad
for the comparison. I was young and only knew
that the sheer synthetic on my legs was always too big,
always riding up. They made my legs paler than
the rest of me and I marveled at how they glowed
white, the ghost of me under my dress.
This was the '90s and early 2000s. We listened
to NSYNC and chased each other on our green lawns
singing to Britney, but wanting to be bad girls
like Christina. The neighbors were 13 and 14
and already so cool, so grown up. They wore lip
gloss and had posters of Justin Timberlake
on the ceiling above their beds. When boys and men
drove through our suburban streets and honked
and ogled and screamed, their father screamed
back *she's not even 16.* I was always afraid
back then. The fear of getting kidnapped,
getting pulled into the unmarked van, getting chased
on the way home from school, getting lost

in the woods. I was afraid of these things
in a way I was not afraid of running and falling
and skinning a knee or getting separated
from my mother in a department store between
rows of long coats. I would part them and walk
from one aisle to the next through these secret pathways
I made for myself—the world closing in around
my absence. I am still afraid. A long time ago
but not that long, back in high school, it was alone
in the dark that a boy, a man, pulled down the neck
of my shirt, lifted my breast out. It was a seamless
motion like wrenching a shoulder from its socket.
It was as easy and natural for him as plucking a pear
from a fruit stand. Another boy, man, young man
was there to marvel at my breast. They both reached out,
greedy. They were young, just boys, just young
men but they knew what men knew: that my body
belonged to them the way they knew women's
bodies belonged to them. Any woman in the street walking
dogs, pushing strollers, shouldering leather briefcases.
This happened outside a house under a porchlight
not far from my house, only an expanse of woods
to separate my door from his. I still wonder
that I could do nothing but stare at my exposed breast,
say nothing. If a man were to drag me into dark under-
brush tomorrow, would I scream? Would my body
make any sound as the world closed in around it?

A list of directives:

step on the dead branch
press down on the almost-hurt

watch night through the canopy of leaves

get on the boat   the plane

open your mouth
form the sounds

learn the words
          here's your new alphabet

memorize your SSN
pay your taxes
greet your neighbor

speak only the right sounds
                    a voice with no inflection
          a voice that doesn't waver

               don't you want your children to fit in

smile for the camera

          you are free to be happy now

Nguyen: Also Known As

win / new-win / your dentists doctors maids tailors manicurists are
my family / are my mother brother father sister cousin niece and
nephew / no matter that I'm the only child / no matter if you can't
pronounce it / in first grade beautiful Mrs. Green had to correct
my rendition of my last name / she wore an emerald against her
chalky neck / she taught me how to arrange those pesky g's and
u's and y's / she could not teach me my own language / how
unnatural living in my throat / a name spoken apologetically
/ a name to trip up telemarketers / a tonal language / center
dipthongs / off-gliding triphthongs / a name to make you falter
and stumble / language not your own / a stranger language
veering across the tongue

MATTHEW OLZMANN

Despite the Kicking of Small Animals

our mayor was popular. Not a weakling
like those other mayors, we boasted as he blasted
a puppy through a white husk of moonlight
and into the cornfield. Breath of fresh air, we shouted
as a piglet soared above the pond.
Real straight shooter; just knows how to get things done.
Squirrel over the football field.
Hedgehog through the stained glass
of St. Joe's north transept.
Look at that glorious leg! we sang as the landscape
wheezed and shifted all around us. The flags
over city hall fluttering in a way that reminded us
of some forgotten motif: our mothers dancing, perhaps,
their long dresses whirling in the wind.
And who knew you could launch a lemur
past the street lights, or an entire colony
of auks the length of Main Street?
Pillar of strength.
Wide blue sky. Sweet little lamb.

ANNETTE OXINDINE

Now That Spring Is Coming, More Decrees

Do not pass a butterfly
unless you tear off a wing.
(Make that "both wings")
Do not read a poem
unless you laugh like a hyena
even if there's a dead mother in it.
(Make that "harder if")
Do not read anything
unless you black out
every third word, except those so loooong
they may as well not be English—
those you must gouge out in a rage
I swear you'll start to feel
for every word, unless I have said it.
Do not look at the sky and think
how blue unless you remember
it was even bluer when I came for you.
Do not walk on new grass
unless you sprinkle it
with gasoline.
Do not talk to strangers
(you know who I mean)
about the weather
(you know what I mean).
Do not forget the matches.
(See above)
Don't worry, I got this.
Do not forget to scream
my name when your clothes first catch.
(Make that "your children's clothes" ??)
(See above)
Don't worry about the fall of a sparrow.
I got those tiny claws
clutching wet cat gut,
chirping *love him, love him,*
love him, love him.

GREGORY PARDLO

For Which it Stands

For a flag! I answered facetiously. A flag of tomorrow,
fluent in fire, not just the whispers, lisps, not just the still there
of powdered wigs, dry winds. Who wants a speckled
drape that folds as easy over smirch as fallen soldier?
This is rhetorical. Like, "What to the Negro
is the fourth of July?" A flag should be stitched with a fuse.

Jefferson said for each generation a flag. Maybe
he said Constitution. I once raised a high-top flag
of my hair, a fist, a leather medallion of the motherland.
I studied heraldry and maniples (which are not
what you might guess), little sails and banners
down to the vane of a feather. Because his kids were
rebel cities my father loved like Sherman. Because
I wanted history I could touch like the flank of a beast.

My wife's people are from San Salvador. They sent us
with a guard, his AK shouldered like a mandolin, among
anil-tinted shawls and jerseys, across tiled and pocked
concrete, and the gated stalls of El Centra. I felt sacred
as a goat there, too, as I did below the Mason-Dixon
where our only protection was the Fourteenth Amendment.

Afraid our Yankee plates would be read aggressive as a Jolly
Roger we rented a compact in Atlanta. Charleston, Savannah,
Montgomery, and after Birmingham we were broke.
Skipped Selma. Slept at B&Bs where my dreams power-
washed layers of footnotes and Februaries, revealing
the surreal sheen of Apollo Creed's trunks, the apocalyptic
Americana of Jacko moonwalking around a tinfoil Buzz
Aldrin planting the corporate ensign. Years passed. I grew

youthless in my dad-pants, but still puffed at pinwheels
and windsocks, launched glyphs of grillsmoke and one day
it came to me, as if commissioned, Theaster Gates's Flag

from old fire hoses, a couple dozen, like vertical blinds, no,
like cabin floorboards of canvas colored rusty, brick dust, some
cheerless drab-and-custard, beside a medley of vespertine
blues, hoses evoking landscapes of sackcloth and gunny,
texture of violence and tongues inflamed by shine, holy ghost.

Ross, Duchamp, Johns, et al., are integrated here with officers
of the peace, their dogs, and, in evidence, their pretend
tumescence Gates has hung to cure like pelts
or strips of jerky.

How did it feel to shield spirit with flesh? I mean,
what did it do to the body, water furry as the arm
of an arctic bear? What thirst did it ignite?

Gates's salute is a torch song, a rhythm
of hues marching over a pentimento of rhyme.
I approve its message, its pledge to birth a nation
of belonging and to teach that nation of the fire
shut up in our bones.

Written By Himself

I was born in minutes in a roadside kitchen a skillet
whispering my name. I was born to rainwater and lye;
I was born across the river where I
was borrowed with clothespins, a harrow tooth,
broadsides sewn in my shoes. I returned, though
it please you, through no fault of my own,
pockets filled with coffee grounds and eggshells.
I was born still and superstitious; I bore an unexpected burden.
I gave birth, I gave blessing, I gave rise to suspicion.
I was born abandoned outdoors in the heat-shaped air,
air drifting like spirits and old windows.
I was born a fraction and a cipher and a ledger entry;
I was an index of first lines when I was born.
I was born waist-deep stubborn in the water crying
                    ain't I a woman and a brother I was born
to this hall of mirrors, this horror story I was
born with a prologue of references, pursued
by mosquitoes and thieves, I was born passing
off the problem of the twentieth century: I was born.
I read minds before I could read fishes and loaves;
I walked a piece of the way alone before I was born.

CRAIG SANTOS PEREZ

Love Poems in the Time of Climate Change: Sonnet XVII

I don't love you as if you were rare earth metals, diamonds,
or reserves of crude oil that propagate war:
I love you as one loves most vulnerable things,
urgently, between the habitat and its loss.

I love you as the seed that doesn't sprout but carries
the heritage of our roots, secured, within a vault,
and thanks to your love the organic taste that ripens
from the fruit lives sweetly on my tongue.

I love you without knowing how, or when, the world will end—
I love you naturally without pesticides or pills—
I love you like this because we won't survive any other way,
except in this form in which humans and nature are kin,
so close that your emissions of carbon are mine,
so close that your sea rises with my heat.

Love Poems in the Time of Climate Change: Sonnet XII

Global woman, waxy apple, record heat,
thick smell of algae, burnt peat and sunset,
what rich nitrogen opens between your native trees?
What fossil fuels does a man tap with his drill?

Loving is a migration with butterflies and refugees,
with overcrowded boats and no milkweed:
loving is a clash of petro-states,
and two bodies detonated by a single drone strike.

Kiss by kiss I walk across your scarred landscape,
your border walls, your dam, your reservations,
until our little extinctions transform into peak oil

and push through the narrow pipelines of our veins,
until we bloom wide, like water hyacinth, until we are
and we are more than a fracture in geologic time.

Thanksgiving in the Anthropocene, 2015

Thank you, instant mashed potatoes, your bland taste
makes me feel like an average American. Thank you,

incarcerated Americans, for filling the labor shortage
and packing potatoes in Idaho. Thank you, canned

cranberry sauce, for your gelatinous curves. Thank you,
Ojibwe tribe in Wisconsin, your lake is now polluted

with phosphate-laden discharge from nearby cranberry
bogs. Thank you, crisp green beans, you are my excuse

for eating dessert later. Thank you, indigenous migrant
workers, for picking the beans in Mexico's farm belt,

may your children survive the journey. Thank you, NAFTA,
for making life so cheap. Thank you, Butterball Turkey,

for the word, butterball, which I repeat all day butterball,
butterball, butterball because it helps me swallow the bones

of genocide. Thank you, dark meat for being so juicy
(no offense, dry and fragile white meat, you matter too).

Thank you, 90 million factory farmed turkeys, for giving
your lives this holiday season. Thank you, factory farm

workers, for clipping turkey toes and beaks so they don't scratch
and peck each other in overcrowded, dark sheds. Thank you,

genetic engineering and antibiotics, for accelerating
their growth. Thank you, stunning tank, for immobilizing

most of the turkeys hanging upside down by crippled legs.
Thank you, stainless steel knives, for your sharpened

edge and thirst for throat. Thank you, de-feathering
tank, for your scalding-hot water, for finally killing the last

still conscious turkeys. Thank you, turkey tails, for feeding
Pacific Islanders all year round. Thank you, empire of

slaughter, for never wasting your fatty leftovers. Thank you,
tryptophan, for the promise of an afternoon nap—

I really need it. Thank you, store bought stuffing,
for your ambiguously ethnic flavor, you remind me

that I'm not an average American. Thank you, gravy,
for being hot-off-the-boat and the most beautiful

brown. Thank you, dear readers, for joining me at this
table. Please hold hands, bow your heads, and repeat

after me: "Let us bless the hands that harvest and butcher
our food, bless the hands that drive delivery trucks

and stock grocery shelves, bless the hands that cooked
and paid for this meal, bless the hands that bind

our hands and force feed our endless mouth.
May we forgive each other and be forgiven."

Masturbation Poem in a Time of Climate Change

> "Caring for myself is not self-indulgence, it is self-preservation,
> and that is an act of political warfare."
>   —Audre Lorde

historic drought.
failed crop yield.
climate denier.
closed borders.
new normal.
austerity.
zero emission.
carbon neutral.
O hope spot,
O Naomi,
O resilience,
O Leo,
O Idle No More,
O Redford,
O seed vault,
O Gore,
O locally sourced,
O Pollan,
O bulk aisle,
O McKibben,
O sustainable,
O Rachel,
O renewable energy,
O Dallas,
O organic produce,
O Ruffalo,
O cage free,
O Shailene,
O free range meat,
O Vandana,
O wild caught fish,
O Winona,
O permaculture,
O Bernie,
O Pacific climate warriors,

O Elon,
O rewilding,
O Nasheed,
O indigenous eco-warriors!
O resurgence!
O sacred Standing Rock!
O rising temperatures!
O rising sea levels!
O long emergency!
O you dirty anthropocene!
O you naughty endangered species!
O you naughty keystone species!
O you naughty charismatic species!
O you naughty vulnerable species!
O 400 parts per million!
O 2 degrees celsius!
O carbon bubble!
O precarity!
O peak oil!
O planetary limit!
O tipping point!
O crisis!
O resource wars!
O extreme weather!
O apocalypse!
O die-off!
O mass extinction!
Oooooo un-patented heirloom seeds ....

XANDRIA PHILLIPS

–Bigly–

"but she stands – bigly – under the unruly scrutiny, stands in the wild weed.

In the wild weed
she is a citizen"
—Gwendolyn Brooks

I am already so cumbersome from the America in me,
          and its execution of the body. I don't dance unless I'm sloshed
to my eyebrows in fermentation. I don't dance until
          I've dammed the barrier between my pelvis and its estrangement
from pleasure. I do often roll my tongue, but only to flute
          my lips and spit cherry seeds a respectable distance away from
me. For so long I wanted to be at least one of the following: a willow spine
          and limbs allowed to drift without syncopation, or a manatee
that sailors escort to an ice skating rink. For those of you in the back
          of your heads, that's a skinny awkward sympathy or a fat
decorative allowance. I've lived in shapes I cannot muster the courage
          to name because they are slanted and curved. An octagon
if you will, there, I said it. These false starts at angular, and these teases
          at curves, these crops I'd rather burn than rotate, these hands,
I've laid hands, I've laid hands on myself when I could not for the foreign
          life of me pull a line of rhythm from my scalp to my toes
without shuddering at my own reverberations.

Elegy for the Living and Breathing

Photographs of people under water make me breathe
      deeper. And sometimes the people aren't

people, but holy embodiments of Atlantic trauma.
      Anything with a face submerged

or squalling vengeance. To be brought down to my
      misery, to silence my anxiety, I gulp into

my lungs' pockets for a few cents of oxygen. Can
      you believe we still have to ask nicely?

Can you believe some of us still drown in our own
      lungs? Today it was a picture of Muhammad

Ali boxing underwater, and because he can no longer
      hold his own breath, I rattle the coins in my

chest. Even exhaling, there is audacity in my lungs.
      We are in need of a plan. Let's meet

somewhere between my sternum and the equator for
      survival lessons. Let's deflate something

that we can all agree is monstrous, and take its air
      inside us. Let's witness an infant kicking

and grabbing through a pool. For those moments she
      believes herself back in utero. The compulsion

within someone who wants only to make it to
      the other side on a single clutch of air.

Social Death: Split-Screen, Rewind

until   the blood coursed like tree roots down their backs
until   I ripped myself out of the car until   the helms crusted
over with sea salt doilies until   I felt against his hardness, a boy
who touched his own cheek like it was made from a moth's wing
until   they shared a mutual knowledge of flesh with sharks until
my throat birthed an elegy until   the Atlantic was a wet first kiss
until   his hand loots my right breast until   they peed and
bled in a sandcastle until   his tongue got hip to mine, got lonely
until   ankles sang a red song, ensnared into chorus until   he
offered me a ride until   an Ashanti was an Ashanti, not a hue or
a fist or gun powder until   I was abandoned in the lap of a night
club until   the gold chattered loud over their skin until   I
pressed a stick of color to my lips until   our hunt until

we savage time as it refuses to move forward until   we fall
asleep in our own limbs

Social Death: Split-Screen, Fast Forward

we fall asleep in our own limbs   before we savage time as it
refuses to move forward   before our hunt   before I
pressed a stick of color to my lips   before the gold chattered
loud over their skin   before I was abandoned in the lap of a
night club   before an Ashanti was an Ashanti, not a hue or a fist
or gun powder   before he offered me a ride   before ankles
sang a red song, ensnared into chorus   before his tongue got hip
to mine, got lonely   before they peed and bled in a sandcastle
before his hand loots my right breast   before the Atlantic was a
wet first kiss   before my throat birthed an elegy   before
they shared a mutual knowledge of flesh with sharks   before I felt
alongside his hardness, a boy who touched his own cheek like it was
made from a moth's wing   before the helms crusted over with
sea salt doilies   before I ripped myself out of the car the blood
coursed like tree roots down their backs

She Makes Me Notice

how much fear I live with
when she finger-taps the car

    owned by a white woman who
clocked us pulling cannabis into

our Black femme bodies on the
steps of a brown stone we didn't

    live in. Or when she tugs on my
coat buttons and pulls my gloved

hand into hers on the bus next to
a man who looks to be as old as

    my grandfather. That fear like
chasing the bottom of a bottle

I wasn't old enough to buy
before dragging my contemporary

    and marginal body to the nearest
disco ball or what passes for one

in the country: the arm flooded
with heroin, a gas tank full of

    sugar, glass shards shinning at
the bottom of the river.

    for Ashley

Kevin Prufer

National Anthem

And the shopping center said, *give me, give me.*

And the moon turning on its pole said, *I love you, you who have so much to give.*

And you said, *darling, if you could just wait in the car for ten minutes and I'll be right out—*

And the sliding doors opened for you like a coat.

Then the car ticked like the contented in the catatonic snow

and the black boys at the bus stop laughed in their hoods until a bus dragged them through the night and away—

And a woman paced beneath the store.

Sometimes, I can hear the nation speak through the accumulation of the suburbs—

Olive Garden and Exxon; Bed, Bath & Beyond, the stars that throw their dimes around us all

until the eyes say *Love* and the streets say *Yes!* and the parking lot

fills with angels blowing past the lines of freezing cars.

You had been inside for longer than you said, and when you reemerged

I went to help you with the bags. *I'm sorry, sorry*—into the cold air— *I couldn't help—*

What was the body but a vessel, and what was the store but another,

larger vessel? The keys sang in my numb fingers. The flag applauded in the wind.

And then I saw that you were smiling up at it.

In a Beautiful Country

A good way to fall in love
is to turn off the headlights
and drive very fast down dark roads.

Another way to fall in love
is to say they are only mints
and swallow them with a strong drink.

Then it is autumn in the body.
Your hands are cold.
Then it is winter and we are still at war.

The gold-haired girl is singing into your ear
about how we live in a beautiful country.
Snow sifts from the clouds

into your drink. It doesn't matter about the war.
A good way to fall in love
is to close up the garage and turn the engine on,

then down you'll fall through lovely mists
as a body might fall early one morning
from a high window into love. Love,

the broken glass. Love, the scissors
and the water basin. A good way to fall
is with a rope to catch you.

A good way is with something to drink
to help you march forward.
The gold-haired girl says, *Don't worry*

about the armies, says, *We live in a time*
full of love. You're thinking about this too much.
Slow down. Nothing bad will happen.

The Art of Fiction

In my vanished youth
I wrote a poem called "Fear of Old Age,"
in which I looked in horror on the frail bodies
of the elderly,
              the spotted hands and looming
decay
      and that poem won a prize, $100
and the chance to read it to a half-full auditorium.

Later, in the parking lot,
a woman I'd then have called
very old told me,
           Someday
you'll understand how your poem has hurt me;
I don't expect you to get it now, but
                  someday.

+

Now and then, the memory returns.

She must, I think, be
              dead by now.
She must be dead by now. And knowing this,
I can't help it: I'm smiling
because I was right to be afraid.

+

Tonight, the internet says
they are shooting cops in Dallas. The cause
is social justice
             and the cops are dying on the street.
Last night, cops were shooting black people in Minneapolis
and Baton Rouge. The cause, then,
was public safety.
           Tomorrow, we will be shooting
children in Cleveland (education), taxi drivers in Boston (traffic)
and little old ladies in St. Louis.

+

When Antonio Holmes (my childhood friend, black)
brought his father's handgun to school,

                        all us boys crowded around.

He took it out of his knapsack

                 and its darkness glimmered.
Antonio let each of us hold it

             awkwardly
before he slipped it back into a paper bag,
and the bag into the knapsack.

             It's cool, I said,
remembering its weight and chill in my hand.
And Antonio smiled. *Cool,* he said.

                And right there,
on the playground,

          that's where the memory ends.

+

(Except all of us but Antonio were white.
This is only a fact,

like the gun in my hand was a fact,
solid and capable.)

+

The emergence of Modern Humans
from the vast networks of ancient hominids
didn't come with our discovery of tools
or even with the development of complex
language.

             Rather, anthropologists now believe,
Modern Humans rose (obliterating
all other intelligent hominid species) because
of our ability to create fictions—

                 That is,
we could imagine unverifiable truths larger than ourselves—
gods, ideals, meaningful co-operations toward abstract
goals—and this allowed us to destroy
each sentient,

and therefore complex,
community we encountered
as we migrated out of Africa to new lands.
This, anthropologists call
                    The Cognitive Revolution.

+

The little old lady who hated my poem
walked toward her car with her husband.
She had entered the poetry contest,
                          but she had not won it.

What she said
                stayed with me—

death hovering over her
like a great crow, flexing its wings, its head
pivoting this way and that
                    as she walked toward her car.

+

This, anthropologists call The Cognitive Revolution:
the fiction of terror and immortality hanging over us
                            diversely meaningful,
five cops dead in the street because
                        how else do you respond
to a construct designed to hold vast numbers of us in fear
of death?
            An old lady trembling toward her great black chariot
and out of my life.
            Tomorrow, Antonio Holmes says,
holding his father's gun,
                they will kill a few more black people.

+

But tonight
            I'm typing my memories on a glowing screen.
Apple is a fiction

        made palpable by our communal agreement
about its existence.
                Apple has workers—
many of them building machines overseas as I write.
It has advertisements.
               Bank accounts. Accountants. A CEO.
But *Apple* itself exists only in our mutual habitation
of its fictional essence.

+

(And the iPhones that recorded the murders
of black men in Minneapolis and Baton Rouge, that uploaded
those images to the web
              where everyone I know saw them,
are concrete expressions of the same fiction
                    we all call *Apple*).

+

Someday,
        she said,
             you will know how your poem has hurt me. Tottering
toward her great black hearse
                 on the far side of the Community Center.

Someday, Antonio says,
             pocketing his father's gun,
you will wonder what became of me. Someday, you will look me up—

+

I am looking into the great glowing screen.
It's like a window I can stick my head through.

If I look long enough, I feel as though I am falling into it,
tumbling through blue force fields.

+

Google,
        a fiction that returns to its disciples
facts:
        In 1988, when we were seventeen years old,
Antonio, pursued by police
                at high speed down Shaker Blvd,
put his head through the windshield
                    and into the telephone pole
that also stopped his car.

+

Now what do you think of that?
                says the old lady from the afterlife.
What do you think of that?
              say those five dead cops
and the two dead black men.
In order to form a more perfect fiction,
              say the anthropologists,
though I can't tell if they're smiling, or not.

Then their cars pull from the Community Center parking lot
and disappear into the night forever—

+

and gentle Antonio walks across the playground
into memory and haze,
            his knapsack slung over one shoulder.

+

The window glows bluely into the black room
where I am forever writing my memories
              on glass.

The Translator

A *poem in translation,*
>   the young man was fond of saying,
is like the dead body of a foreigner
>   *washed up on our shores.*
>   Here
he usually paused to let the metaphor sink in.

Some members of the audience nodded thoughtfully.

I will now read from my translations of a little-known ancient Roman poet,
he told them,
>   shuffling his papers, then looking into
>   the dark,
half-empty auditorium.

+

The dead body refused to be still. The waves
loved it too much,
>   pushing it onto the beach, then rolling it
seaward again.
>   And so it made its way down the beach,
alighting for a moment
>   or several moments,
>   on the wet sand,
then bobbing out
>   among the American swimmers.

+

120 foreigners in a leaking boat
is too many,
>   so the ocean fills with poems. Some retain
the qualities of their original language,
>   but others sink blackly
into a new language.

+

Here I am, out here! I can see your
oil rigs glittering on the horizon,
        says the young woman whom no one
listens to. Or,
      she says nothing,
clinging to the side of the waterlogged boat,
where she has floated all night
       among the drifting bodies.

A few of them became tangled among the oil rigs,
while others arrived
      gently on our shore.

+

A poem that has floated some distance
from its accident
     transforms—so the swimmers
ran away in horror
     when at last he came to rest
on a crowded part of the beach.

+

You foreigners in your many-sailed ships,
come join the empire! the translator intones
     from his spot-lit podium,
and the audience sighs.
    Here I am, out here,
says a little voice in the translation,
    a voice no one,
not even the translator,
    can hear.

+

The audience
had come to hear a lecture on poetry in translation

and now the translator was going on
about the ancient Roman tendency to absorb,
and therefore transform,
                        foreign cultures,
their gods and foods.

Outside the auditorium, it had grown dark,
a perfect summer night.
                        The thousand vessels
on the great black ocean
glittered and loomed

+

                        and for days, bodies
washed up on the beach.
                        Now, the American workers
zippered them into vinyl bags,

which, in the translator's metaphor,
constitutes a kind of publication.

+

 But what is there to say
                        about that young woman
still clinging to the wreckage
two days into my poem?
                        A gentle summer rain
prickles her skin. *Here I am,* she says,
looking toward the oil rigs hunkering between her
and the shore.
                  Here I am.

+

She is a very fine woman
and someone should translate her.

The Mexicans

The kitten
crawled under the dashboard
to the engine

so the young woman pulled over
and pressed her head
against the steering wheel.

The radio was talking about
fifty-one dead Mexicans
in a locked and airless truck.

Sleet needled the windshield,
the hood iced shut,
and she was afraid to turn the engine back on.

Then onrushing snow,
so what could she do on a back road
three hundred miles from home,

everything she owned in the U-Haul trailer,
the push of cold wind,
night coming on,

and no sound from under the hood
where her kitten had crawled.

+

In my nation's fever dream our fences are nothing

to the Mexicans, who clamber over dressed like us,

in my nation's dreams they arrive on black trains

cutting through the desert nights, incognito in their seats,

the passing towns make their faces glow, the Mexicans

dangle from parachutes in black skies singing

as the airplanes fade, oh, Mexicans in our fields, Mexicans

on rooftops, the helicopters spit your ropes over us—

+

The kitten
curled on the warm engine block
heard her calling
but wouldn't move,

and *I don't know where I am,*
she said into her phone.
I don't know where I am,

and *what am I supposed to do?*
If I start the car—

+

Mexicans flitting through sleet-wet woods
in my nation's dream,

as the young woman sits in her car's lit cab
and the radio, voicebox of my sleeping people, says,
an airless space, says, *more after the break,*

and then they emerge
from the black trees
along the winter roadside
where she's stopped her car—

+

You have to turn the engine on,
                              her father told her.
She'd kept the heaters on, the battery was probably half-dead,

snow piled on the hood, blotting out the woods.
You can't just wait all night,
                                        you have to get back on the road—

+

The distant highway rumbled
                                        with trucks,
the Wal-Mart parking lot thick with trucks,
a rest stop and a long black row of locked trucks,
and the low motel like a clot, dead trucks
under the sodium lights,
                                        black truck and a little voice inside it—

+

The Mexicans floated down like snow.
The news descended
                                        from the blinking satellite
like the Mexicans,
                                        right into the radio,
while the wind disturbed the bushes
                                        like Mexicans
rustling past, emerging now, like Mexicans,

where the crying young woman
in the cooling, snow-capped car
didn't notice them at all,
                                        and the radio spoke on and on.

+

When the engine had cooled completely,
the kitten, at last, slipped from the engine block,
and dropped to the floor by her feet.
                                        Such a relief,
she told her father on the phone, easing onto the road,
everything's fine, fine,

                    the rumble of the U-Haul,
the kitten in its box on the seat beside her.

+

(Mexicans at the woods' edge
watching the receding taillights,
in the obliterating snow—)

(A young man stepped into
the back of a dark truck,

wrapped in the sound
of fifty people breathing—)

Cruelties

A young man behind the garage spraying a wasps' nest
until the wasps grow heavy and dumb
dripping from the gutter
      and still he sprays
until their curled black bodies decorate the woodpile
and the nest drips poison
        while the young man smiles
is one kind of cruelty

and the cargo ship's captain throwing the castaways overboard
and though they wave their arms and call to him
he picks them off
     one by one
and only when the last one slips below her bloodcloud
does he lower his revolver
       to bow to the applauding crew
is another kind of cruelty

There is something to admire in the first cruelty
it is necessary and cultivating
       I tell myself
having moved on to the garden now
pouring poison over the fire ants' mound
spraying the hibiscus the snails were eating

but someone recorded the second cruelty on a cell phone
he'd later lose in a Bangkok taxi
so someone else could upload that video to the web
where we'd all watch it happen
       again and again and

thank God my cruelties are small
it is impossible to tell where those stowaways died
the sea is wide open
      there are so many people
think of the cargo ships the shipping containers
         the economies
bright and featureless—wireless—best now
to close up the shed
      the garden is perfect
it is a perfect garden

DEAN RADER

America I Do Not Call Your Name Without Hope

after Neruda

America I do not call your name without hope
not even when you lay your knife
against my throat or lace my hands
behind my back, the cuffs connecting
us like two outlaws trying to escape
history's white horse, its heavy whip
a pistolshot in the ear. Lost land,
this is a song for the scars on your back,
for your blistered feet and beautiful
watch, it is for your windmills, your
magic machines, for your fists. It
is for your wagon of blood, for your dogs
and their teeth of fire, for your sons
and the smoke in their hearts. This is for
your verbs, your long lurk, your whir.
This is for you and your fear, your tar,
for the white heat in your skin and
for your blue bones that one day may sing.
This is for your singing. This is for the past,
but not for what's passed. This is for daybreak
and backbreak, for dreams and for darkness.
This song is not for your fight, but it is a song
for fighting. It is a song of flame but not for burning.
It is a song out of breath but a plea for breathing.
It is the song I will sing when you knock
on my door, my son's name in your mouth.

STELLA VINITCHI RADULESCU

like history a poem

> "I, too, sing America.
> I am the darker brother."
> —Langston Hughes

cats sleep
close the door to the attic

the noise comes from my mouth
straight talk & sounds

of rage

humans drinking human
blood

& monsters wear the crown
In God we Trust

I am caged in words
like history:

voices, you, don't shiver
bury the corpses

the Evil   my yellow shoes—
yellow for the eternal

walk   the TV zoom zoom

barbarians on the road
my neighbors hanging their clothes

the sun &
the clothes line   lines

lines—
disruption in time don't blink
stay tuned
keep thinking   fill up the void

a syllable is worth a life
& drink their milk babies are coming

babies like stones   hey, joy
you've lost your *y*

: a strike in Heaven   Dante
says is divine

JULIAN RANDALL

The Search for Frank Ocean or a Brief History of Disappearing

"Fucking pig get shot, 300 men will search for me"
—Frank Ocean

A drought does not name itself
in anything but the splintering
of skin into a series of wanting
rivers and the cities that gave
all that water a name as if it
were kin   as if July were not
slow piano and crimson
all over the street   and I guess
you could call this a war
in the way only who can be seen
is alive and maybe not even that

•

August prepares its heavy gown
for our shoulders and I have
nothing to sing   but the heat
on the screen   two trends
#BatonRougePolice
       #WheresTheAlbumFrank

•

Happy June 222nd
       Happy anniversary Frank
              Maybe Frank was never even there
This album definitely not done
       Frank need to come home
       This gay ass nigga gonna break our hearts again
       All I want is a song
                     This nigga a lie
              He fix his mouth   and nothing spills out
Frank might be dead y'all

Frank might be dead y'all
    Another nigga gone missing
        Happy June 225th
                I swear he never coming back
I swear I saw him
            I swear it's been Summer for 3 years

                    •

A name is something you surrender
in parts   if you are lucky
        I am not
much more beyond that
which traces the borders of me
into a bed in mid-July
        I am not
much more than my secrets

                    •

Boy say Bi_____
and his tongue splits

Boy say Bi_____
and his mouth is public property

Boy say Bi_____
and belongs nowhere

Boy say Bi_____
and now none of his gods
return his calls

                    •

A body gets silent
and it is either haunted
or will be

A body gets silent
and everyone can sing it dead

A body gets silent
and we name it after the silence
to forget it was ever a boy

Silence inundates my throat
there is more than one way
to have a boy in your mouth

•

The body is a glass home
I am somewhere I used to live
fragile and nearly translucent
opaque only where smoke tongues
me into the illusion of shelter
I shatter/into more/me

CAMILLE RANKINE

Aubade

They say brave but I don't want it.
Who will we mourn today. Or won't we.

Black all the windows. Lower
down the afternoon. I barricade

all my belonging. I am mostly never real
American or anything

availing. But I do take. And take
what's given. The smell of blood.

I breathe it in. The dirt so thick with our good
fortune. And who pays for it. And what am I

but fear, but wanting. I'll bite
the feeding hand until I'm fed

and buried. In the shining day.
All deadly good

intentions. A catalogue of virtues.
This is how I'll disappear.

ALEXANDRA LYTTON REGALADO

La Mano

*For the more than 60,000 children from Central America who cross
the border unaccompanied.*

With lines from Maya Angelou and Richard Wilbur

Arcing above our apartment building,
        above the rousing city and green skirts
of the San Salvador volcano, a flock
        of wild parakeets comes to roost
outside our window; my nine-month son
        rests his head on my chest and all I want
is to draw the curtains, but he's coughed
        all night and now his breathing
is slow, near sleep, though his eyes snap open
        with each squawk. I imagine the parakeets
preening their emerald feathers, joyful in their ceremony
        of clacks and trills. They are not musing
the capriciousness of nature as I am; they don't know
        five thirty am, only that the sun has tinged
the mountainsides gold and that this alcove echoes
        their welcome beautifully. The wild parakeets tap
at the windowpane and my son stirs,
        raises his sleep-etched face to mine.
Together we slip past the curtain and discover
        seven green parakeets, perhaps a little smaller,
their feathers scruffier than I had envisioned.
        Two squabble over a prime niche and the stronger
one comes towards the glass, wings unfurled,
        fat tongue thrusting from his open beak. I want
to unlatch the window and sprinkle seed, lure them
        to perch on our shoulders and arms, anything
to make them stay longer. Instead, my son, rooted in
        the things unknown but longed for still—
greets them with the slap of an open palm to the windowpane,
        and in a clapping of wings
they leap from the narrow corridor at once, a raucous fleeing,
        with headlong and unanimous consent,
a disappearing stain, a distant murmuration
        swallowed from sight.

ALBERTO RÍOS

We Are of a Tribe

We plant seeds in the ground
And dreams in the sky,

Hoping that, someday, the roots of one
Will meet the upstretched limbs of the other.

It has not happened yet.
We share the sky, all of us, the whole world:

Together, we are a tribe of eyes that look upward,
Even as we stand on uncertain ground.

The earth beneath us moves, quiet and wild,
Its boundaries shifting, its muscles wavering.

The dream of sky is indifferent to all this,
Impervious to borders, fences, reservations.

The sky is our common home, the place we all live.
There we are in the world together.

The dream of sky requires no passport.
Blue will not be fenced. Blue will not be a crime.

Look up. Stay awhile. Let your breathing slow.
Know that you always have a home here.

The Border: A Double Sonnet

The border is a line that birds cannot see.
The border is a beautiful piece of paper folded carelessly in half.
The border is where flint first met steel, starting a century of fires.
The border is a belt that is too tight, holding things up but making it
    hard to breathe.
The border is a rusted hinge that does not bend.
The border is the blood clot in the river's vein.
The border says *stop* to the wind, but the wind speaks another language,
    and keeps going.
The border is a brand, the "Double-X" of barbed wire scarred into the
    skin of so many.
The border has always been a welcome stopping place but is now a Stop
    sign, always red.
The border is a jump rope still there even after the game is finished.
The border is a real crack in an imaginary dam.
The border used to be an actual place, but now, it is the act of a thousand
    imaginations.
The border, the word *border*, sounds like *order*, but in this place they do
    not rhyme.
The border is a handshake that becomes a squeezing contest.

The border smells like cars at noon and wood smoke in the evening.
The border is the place between the two pages in a book where the spine
    is bent too far.
The border is two men in love with the same woman.
The border is an equation in search of an equals sign.
The border is the location of the factory where lightning and thunder
    are made.
The border is "NoNo" the Clown, who can't make anyone laugh.
The border is a locked door that has been promoted.
The border is a moat but without a castle on either side.
The border has become Checkpoint *Chale*.
The border is a place of plans constantly broken and repaired and broken.
The border is mighty, but even the parting of the seas created a path,
    not a barrier.
The border is a big, neat, clean, clear black line on a map that does
    not exist.
The border is the line in new bifocals: below, small things get bigger;
    above, nothing changes.
The border is a skunk with a white line down its back.

Border Lines

A weight carried by two
Weighs only half as much.

The world on a map looks like the drawing of a cow
In a butcher's shop, all those lines showing
Where to cut.

That drawing of the cow is also a jigsaw puzzle,
Showing just as much how very well
All the strange parts fit together.

Which way we look at the drawing
Makes all the difference.
We seem to live in a world of maps:

But in truth we live in a world made
Not of paper and ink but of people.
Those lines are our lives. Together,

Let us turn the map until we see clearly:
The border is what joins us,
Not what separates us.

ALISON C. ROLLINS

The Beastangel

after Robert Hayden's "Bone-Flower Elegy"

In the dream I enter him
I   the eater of numbers
the black-lipped barcode
of cost have come for him
because he owes me. He
owes me the broken machine
the bone structure gone limp
over leg of time. I   irreverent
as safe sex breathlessly
whispering this is not a threat
but a promise for the love of
the wolf on lockdown. Why
the long face? the horsefly
asked the muzzle as though to
suggest these mouths we
have are traps, bold-faced lairs
of brotherhood. Cover your eyes
and you'll miss it, you'll miss this
squalid city growing legs from its
scalp. His kneecaps jerked beneath
the sheet, skinned eyelids rolling back
to the/   Point to where he touched
you on the doll, he asked.
¿cómo se dice "everywhere"?
He will pay for this, the heroic
antihero announced, the vulture-
masked man surveying the damage
the clinical centaur now spooked
his hind legs reared as if to say
demons fear beasts in twos.
Rage bound tight in synthetic
skin/   bound and ridden in dialect

at an angle of consumption. After
feeding he asks, What's the damage?
The legless caterpillar humping itself
forward/   toward my mouth, rending
the lip a cleft palate, twisted up from
firegold sand, a habit of creature
malformed. The men laid flowers
on my mother's tongue, they come
see about me. These flowers are edible
men/   flowers of sawtooth bone.

Why Is We Americans

We is gator teeth hanging from the rear-
view mirror as sickle cells suckle at Big
Momma's teats. We is dragonfly
choppers hovering above Walden Pond.
We is spinal cords shedding like the skin
of a cottonmouth. We is Psalm 23 and
the Pastor's chattering chicklets. We is
a good problem to have. We is throats
constricting and the grape juice
of Jesus. We is Roach and Mingus in
Birdland. We is *body electric,* eyes
watering with moonshine, glossy lips
sticky with lard. We is half brothers in
headlock, arm-wrestling in the dirt.
We is Vaseline rubbed into knocked
knees and cracked elbows. We is ham
hocks making love to kidney beans. We
is Orpheus, lute in hand, asking *do we
have a problem?* We is the backstory
of myth. We is sitting horse and crazy
bull. We is brown paper bags and
gurgled belches. We is hooded ghosts
and holy shadows roaming Mississippi
goddamned. We is downbeats and
syncopation's cousin. We is mouths
washed out with the blood of the lamb.
We is witch-hazel-coated backs sucking
on peppermint wrappers. We is the
spiked antennas of a triangle face
praying mantis. We is barefoot
tongue-tied hogs with slit throats and
twitching bellies. We is sun tea and
brewed bitches. We is the crying
pussies that stand down when told to
man up. We is Radio Raheem and Zoot
Suit Malcolm. We is spit-slick low cuts
and fades. We is scrappy black-masked
coons and turkey-necked bullfrogs. We
is the pits of arms at stake, the clouds

frothing at the mouth. We is swimmers
naked, private parts allegedly fondled
by Whitman beneath the water. We is
late lurkers and castrated tree limbs
on the Sunday before last. We is red-
veined pupils and piss-stained knickers,
slack-jawed and slumped in the
bathroom doorway. We is whiplash
and backhanded ways of settling grief.
We is clubbin' woolly mammoths
upside the head, jammin' fingers in
Darwin's white beard. We is comin'
round yonder, pigeon-toed and
bowlegged, laughin' our heads off.
We is lassoed cowboys swingin' in
the sweet summer breeze.

Liz Rosenberg

To the President Elect

May you be kind till the end
of your brief reign as king.
Others have come and gone, leaving
a bitter taste behind.
Others left nothing at all.
Oh, show us how to work
and to be kind, which is to say,
let us learn how to pray like the old
sardonic Jews—
"May God save and keep the tsar…
Far from us!"
May you turn back.
May you grow up at last.
Listen:
Help us
to change our minds.

The Real True President Asleep

Not that sad clown, but this one behind the scenes—
I want to shake his brass hand,
watch him burst onto the twisting staircase
of America after blood-soaked
days when he broods over the dead
too heavy to move, thinking how can this go on?
He rolls like a thundercloud across the Midwest
and thrusts his lightning fork deep in the South,
he breaks together the heads of the North and East
and bends over the boiling fountain of the volcano to drink.
I have seen the nations gather round him.
England meets him in the garden secretly,
Russia touches his pocket.
China turns her back and stares covertly at the horizon.

He is the angel of death ascending toward God
to settle about the immortal soul
with an excuse and a million complaints;
he thinks people are laughing whenever his back is turned.
What has all his strength brought him if he still must contend
with his own mean moods and ugly drunks?
His gold limbs are too heavy to lift
and his jeweled eyes snap shut on a premonition—
this Councilor who can sense his enemies asleep
and knows what they are dreaming;
who hovers over the broken roofs of houses,
their sad snows in winter and short summer hours,
who peeks into lit apartments
and laughs at the tv show hysterically laughing back,
who longs for peace and friendly feeling
and can circle the globe forever
with his loneliness and hunger violently drumming.
He bears it up in darkness and he throws it down in darkness
to the ordinary man of state, this imposter, who lies
sleeping with his troubled gilt head resting on a mirror.

NICOLE SANTALUCIA

Thumping in Central Pennsylvania

The cows and apple trees and tractor trailers
thump between the prison yard and the university.
Sometimes I chase a herd of cows out of my classroom
and the earth thumps. The word of the lord thumps.
The word thump breaks my ribs. Brown battery operated
cows thump through traffic. Factories thump and farmers
thump. The warehouses are full of thumps. The sky thumps
to the ground when I get home from work and kiss my wife.
When two women fall asleep in the same bed
the stars thumpthumpthumpthumpthump
like bullets that have been hovering
over our heads since the beginning of time.

Supermarket Blowout

There are fruit-shaped guns
at the supermarket:
the apples have triggers,
the avocados bullets,
the extra, large barrel-bananas
are discounted on Tuesday
when you buy two bunches.
The grenades are nestled
next to the black grapes
and the green grapes
expand on impact.
Once a month
there's a "Blowback" sale
and day-old fruit-guns
are free after 7pm.
I can't face it:
we are running low on
apple-shaped apples
and avocado-shaped avocados.
The handgun-oranges,
AR-15-grapefruits,
and pistol-pomelos
are always two-hundred dollars off
in the weekly flyer.
The corn in aisle nine pops
when you pay
with your NRA Visa.
In the gun-shaped produce section
there's a raffle for the 20-gauge-melon-
pump-action with a 26-inch barrel.
To enter, all you have to do
is show up and say, *I hate gays.*

After the Voting Polls Closed

My heart is over there next to burrito wrappers
splattered like a ketchup packet from the gas station,
a little packet of tomato paste
and corn syrup that's been stepped on.
The crows peck at my heart with their warrior scarred beaks
and hop into a dumpster where broken glass,
bullet shells, votes, and women gather.
The crows collect emptiness,
fly by metal hangers in the trees:
the clanks echo survival.

When there's no place to call home
the crows teach us how to build nests
with garbage, desperation, and ash.
The people turn to one another and ask,
Did you hear about the crows that make nests out of fire?
Or, *Did you know that crows remember your face?*

It's November and I refuse to suffer.
The crows know what it is like to belong,
yet they choke on silence and caw in emptiness.

I've been trying to stuff myself into an empty soda bottle
that's been tossed out of a car window
and suction cupped to the ground
by a pile of wet leaves behind a dumpster
in the parking lot that emptied out
after the voting polls closed.

If I could just fit into a plastic, green tinted soda bottle,
I would squeeze through the small mouth hole
and look at a fuzzy, discolored world from the gutter.

sam sax

Doctrine

the time for nuance is over
i argue over breakfast
explaining how it's oft used
to confuse dissent—knife
through my poached egg.
politicized work made all yolky,
easy to consume & forget.
i dab with the toasted bread
agitation & propaganda i rant
is the only just path for artists
gesturing with my utensils
heavenward. i've said a lot
of things which in retrospect
would've been better
had i kept my mouth shut.
i once said something to a friend
i won't repeat here
& now she's no longer my friend.
i'll never forget what her eyes did
as i finished speaking
stones in a bucket.
words have consequences
they're both material & reveal
the spirit that speaks them.
what i meant over breakfast
is the time's too urgent for work
that doesn't have blood in it.
what i meant is insurgency
is our birthright, that nuance
comes from the french meaning
to *shade*—why another painting
of a lake when there's so much
rage boiling outside the canvas?
what does it mean i don't mean
what i say when i say it? i don't know

what i mean. silence is golden
& gold's the standard measurement
for capital. the golden rule is do
unto others as you would have them
do unto you. but what when they do
you ugly first as they always
seem to? i finish my coffee &
it's political whether i want it
to be or not.

LAUREN MARIE SCHMIDT

In Defense of Poetry

The Haven House for Homeless Women and Children

To you who say

poetry is a waste of ten homeless mothers' time—
that I should correct their grammar and spelling,
spit-shine their speech so it gleams, make them sound
more like me, that I should set a bucket of *Yes, Miss,*
Thank You, and *Whatever you say, Miss* on their heads,
fill that bucket heavy, tell them how to tip-toe
to keep it steady, that I should give them something
they can truly use, like diapers, food, or boots—

I say

you've never seen these women lower their noses
over poetry, as if praying the rosary, as if hoping
for a lover to slip his tongue between their lips,
or sip a thin spring of water from a fountain.

Welfare Mothers

The Haven House for Homeless Women and Children

LaQuita was chewing her cuticles when I noticed
how thin she had become, so careworn and thin. This afternoon,
her face was not its usual honey-gold, but gray—her hips thin,
    wrists thin, all over thin. I asked her if she'd eaten today,
and with pink-rimmed eyes fixed on her fingers she shook her head.

I pulled eight singles from my jeans, bills as soft and worn
as used tissues, and held them out for her to take to the Wawa at the corner.
She held the money in a stiff gaze, but did not move until I took her wrist,
    pressed the slim fold in her palm, and closed her fingers around it.
She returned with two bagels, a convenience store coffee,

a cherry Gatorade, a plastic knife, and one small cup of cream cheese.
I waited for the honey to return to her face as she ate and ate and ate.
With the last lump of food still stuffed inside her cheek,
    LaQuita approached to give me a wrinkled Wawa receipt
and drop a dime, a nickel, and two pennies in my hand.

Unto Others

To the roomful of people at the private fundraiser for Mitt Romney, May 2012

"There are 47 percent who are with [the President], who are dependent upon government, who believe that they are victims, who believe that government has a responsibility to care for them, who believe that they are entitled to health care, to food, to housing, to you name it....That's entitlement."
—Mitt Romney

"All things therefore whatsoever ye would that men should do unto you, even so do ye also unto them."
—Matthew 7:12

"Who is here so vile that will not love his country? If any, speak; for him have I offended."
—Julius Caesar, Act II, scene ii

Who there knows how good it is to know
a warm bed and a roof? If any, speak.

Who there knows how good it is to know
a schoolroom? If any, speak.

Who there knows how good it is to know
the stiffness of new shoes? If any, speak.

Who there knows how good it is to know
the steam of a meal on your cheeks? If any, speak.

Who there knows how good it is to know
some God hears you weep? If any, speak.

Who there knows how good it is to know?
All of you know, so speak.

Say you know how good it is to know.
All of you know, so speak. Say it's OK

for others to know how good it is to know.
Say it. Speak. You lose nothing

if others know how good it is to know.
Go ahead. Speak.

If you know how good it is to know,
why then don't you speak?

Why then don't you speak?
Say something. Speak. Speak. Speak.

The Fourth of July

If I hadn't been sitting on my mother's lap,
I don't know that she could have smacked
out the orange embers that singed the sleeve

of my zip-up in time, before my jacket
went up in a wicked flame and our yearly
block-party-with-firecrackers-and-hot-dogs fun

at the Marcazie's turned tragic. And even though
she did smother the burns on my hoodie,
those were the days I was afraid of fireworks—

the pop they made when lit, the hiss as they soared
through the sky, the crack and bang, the way
even the softest summer wind would lift smoke

over our houses, our heads, the way ash trickled down
on our upturned faces, shiny with that great
and colorful light. I especially feared the ones

that released an almost animal scream as they scattered
in inestimable directions, the way we kids fled
from behind bushes playing Man Hunt in the after-

fireworks dark. Only a game of hide-and-seek,
but the stinging belts of terror in the chase
were as real as the scrapes on our knees

when we fell under the weight of the enemy
hands that crashed too heavily on our shoulders
in the tag. The next day, we'd find firecracker husks,

small round trunks, cluttering our lawns,
floating in our pools, flattened in the street
by Converse sneakers or cars. We found a cat

like that once, whipped by speeding wheels
and left behind. Not dead, but almost,
because, in those days—

when we played Contra and Commando
on our Ataris, when we tied yellow ribbons
around trees in our schoolyard, sang the revival

of "God Bless the U.S.A." for our parents' flashing
cameras, when we wore buttons on our chests
that said, *Support Our Troops*—

Mrs. Marcazie hoarded cats, and droves
of underfed beasts swarmed our streets,
scoured the dumpsters behind the apartments

for something forgotten to eat. Sometimes
they collapsed sideways from exhaustion.
Once, one of the big kids tried to plug the asshole

of a stray with a firecracker, but she screamed,
swiped straight for his eyes, and corkscrewed
out of his grip. Bounding away, she was

the amber flicker of light I sucked into a bowl
of weed the night the boys in my senior class
stuffed a firecracker into watermelon flesh

in the parking lot behind the Tom Sawyer Diner.
Peter dashed away from the pop of the lit fuse
and hopped into the Buick. Almost midnight

at the all-night eatery, we watched flesh splatter,
the spray of red wet fanning out from the round belly
of the fruit. Shards of the green-and-white-lined rind

dropped with the weight of a cat's paws. We cackled
as only kids can and careened away in our cars, waving
at the owner who flipped us off from the emergency exit door.

Tonight, more than twenty years and four wars later,

in the middle of another war, I join my neighbors
on our beach street. We wait in anticipation for the show,
for that first pop and hiss, that scarlet crack

of light in the sky, and when the blasts begin,
together, we gaze upwards, our eyes agog,
ice cream cones dripping down our knuckles.

The Social Worker's Advice

The Haven House for Homeless Women and Children

Jabbing a finger at my face, you say, *You can't have
empathy. Empathy will eat you alive,* as if empathy
were a beast with feathers, fur, and hair, with hind legs
and deft feet, wings and claws, a beast that soars,
stalks, lunges, springs, a beast that chases, a beast
that screams instead of sings, with giant jaws
and a tongue budded with a rapacious taste for fools
like me, fools who don't believe the beast exists to eat,
who let it burrow its snout between our legs, fingers,
up to our armpits—the spaces of our common human stink.

But you see a beast that sniffs and snarls for a thick blue vein
to sic, and when I look at you I understand the beast more plainly—
I see that its skin collects pock marks each time you dock
merit points to teach the mothers not to "talk Black,"
I see that its forehead sprouts a thousand of your scornful eyes,
its claws slash as swift and deep as your condescension—

because what you mean is that I can't have empathy
for these girls, for times like these, for a place like this,
for Nicole who tallies the number of days it's been
since she last flushed her veins with a spoon-cooked mix,
twenty-eight days and counting. No empathy
for Nicole because she can never seem to find
matching socks for her four-year-old son, or because
she folds flowers from twice-used computer paper
to calm her nerves. Bouquets of paper daisies
sprout from vases on all four tables in the dining room.

What you mean is that I can't have empathy for Takina,
who was told to go by Tina because her white, adoptive
mother—middle-aged, middle-classed—prefers it.
Her birth-mother is five years gone and Tina-Takina
thinks she might be pregnant again. I can't have empathy

for Denice who is pregnant with her third, but didn't know
until she was too far in, for Angelica who fell down the stairs
while holding her infant son, too spent from pre-sun
feedings and weeping in the wee hours as minutes lurch by.
Each tick-tock is the sound of the dead-locked door
of the nighttime aide who snores in the small room
near the exit like a beast at the gates, preventing escape
from this place, this time, from lives like these
without signing a release form for the Division of Youth
and Family Services, like Dionna, who took her two kids
to a hotel where, alone, at night, she stares at ceiling holes
in the red glow of the word VACANCY flashing through
windows with no curtains. I can't have empathy for LaQuita,
so thin that when she aims her breast at her baby's lips,
she prays she has something wet and real to give.

When you say, with your wagging finger, *You can't have*
empathy. Empathy will eat you alive, what you mean
is that I can't have empathy for these girls, and when I look
at you, I cannot help but wonder when you first believed
empathy would do more than sniff and lick your palms.

So, I say, let it take me, then, this beast of your invention,
let it slip its fangs into my skin and tear through my throat,
let it suck all the fat and blood from off my solid bones.

Raena Shirali

Dare I Write It

dare i the greenery flashing by hallucinatory out the window,
parents in the front seat yelling back at me
for wearing a hollister skirt, for cursing
in front of a group of younger indian boys. do i dare
my salwar-clad grandmother at middle school PTA meetings. do i dare
parents, their skin dark around the eyes, darker than some of the other
     kids' parents—
mom hands me salt scrub & a loofah, says, *get to work.* dare i work
on my tan, skin without sunscreen, dare i explain to a friend
the back of my neck, dare i explain that i am not a "nigger."
dare i use the word. dare i understand *i should not be using this word.*
my friend shakes her dirty blonde hair back & forth slowly:
ain't a difference. dare i know if you put the word "sand" before,
she's right; my people apparently live surrounded by sand, never mind
     the river,
the himalayas, never mind dharavi & the mountains of sheet metal
& laundry my dad says he once was assigned to during his residency.
says it was electrical & no plumbing & would you look at that,
not a grain of sand in sight. how can i argue
with a question like that—how can i answer *will you have an arranged
     marriage*
when i'm thirteen—how justify—how rectify—how peel off
epidermis & then dermis & then how rid oneself of a name:
i don all the popped collars, all the pink crop tops,
by God, whom i now presumably believe in, i will show my tits
to the neighborhood boys so they shut up about the sand, so they stop
chasing me down in their pickup trucks yelling *run, nigger run* until i turn
to face & correct them: *SAND-nigger.* dare i sit on the roof of a brick house
with white girls & laugh when they laugh at that story. dare i
coat my eyes in black. dare i chameleon. dare i write. dare i girl.

Between Here & Predictable Characters

Watching *Friends* because my mother once forbade it, I am on the
  phone listening
to a woman unchanged. She says, *uh, yeah, of course we didn't let you
  watch that,*
like I've grown up to be the kind of twenty-five-year-old who dates
  around & hates the idea
of marriage. Insert laugh track here. I can only hope my mother means
she wouldn't want me watching a show where all the characters
aren't brown, where not a single one knows *henna* and *mehndi*
mean the same thing, where men come in & out of bedrooms
like small phantoms during the day. Men are always leaving
my room without taking or leaving anything. It would be such stupid
poetry to call them phantoms. Phoebe asks why no one has ever considered
that human existence might be too big for us to fathom. My mother
doesn't want to talk about this right now. Rachel has sex
with her ex in a dentist chair. I have sex with my ex
more places than I can count, & we both feel like shit
the next day, & I feel like shit even now, even here. What did I miss
having not seen these mishaps? Ross confesses he has loved Rachel
  since ninth grade
& that same year I held my own breasts in my hands and wondered
who will ever want these? I am so lost in this episode.
God, I tell my roommate, *this is F.O.B. as shit of me,* & I'm right,
aren't I, my brown body swaddled in my own charso, my mother
alone while states away my father teaches whole stadiums how the heart
  works,
both of us staring into tungsten screens, wishing anything had taught us
how to live in this moment.

SCHEREZADE SIOBHAN

second generation

who wants to leave / home? / who wants to end / with a skull
full of sand / skin bleached to salt / I will never breathe / in the
opium-dusk of kabul / my grandfather prays / for a simple death /
a door / closing quietly. a lilac / light murmuring / under the
jacarandas / here is an afternoon / where / the crows circle our
courtyard / in a carcanet of black jaspers / here is a room / where
/ the hours / slowly undress into years / & we have no way of
knowing / when / the days will become / their own doppelgängers
/ when we will begin / to remember / what didn't happen / the
beginning of all / ache is not loss / but speech. if i stay silent / i
refuse / to confess that pain / has mothered me longer / than the
possibility / of a person / before you come to a body / you already
are a ghost / i jot a silhouette / in my diary / canary a yellow /
sunglow a marigold / above the amygdala / spend the night
petaling / the origami of my brain / sometimes the sheer act of /
waking is a war / my mouth hides more / violence than the iris-
blue / belly of any ocean / i mute the news / howling / about the
residue of refugees / as if people were dust / waiting to settle /
where we shouldn't / yesterday i / woke up and searched / for a
nylon rope / my neck cracking / its own trestle / today i / brought
home a maggot-festooned stray / tomorrow? / tomorrow is not my
animal to tame / not my amnesia to name / in the mango-ripening
heat / i sit with a handicapped dog / snoring in my lap / &
ask / what borders did you draw / out of your scars / that you grew
so foreign / in your own skin? / enough / is a reason too / i
can't *unhome* myself / (not enough) / look shorewards & pray that
/ a home is where the heart / goes back to whole

CLINT SMITH

Pangaea

after Hanif Abdurraqib

Imagine each continent a splintered
tessellation of wayward fragments.
Each mass of land attempting to
jostle itself free. Pangaea was the last
of the supercontinents, a mass of land
that came together & broke itself apart
several times before. It should come
as no surprise, don't we all find
ourselves coming back to something
we can lose ourselves inside of? Can
we blame the desert for missing the
breeze that tumbles across the grassland?
Can we blame the tundra for a desire to
witness the wrestling of pines? Just the
other day, a bomb killed seventy people
in Pakistan & no one around me heard
a sound. These days, I find myself
blaming Pangaea for the sounds I cannot
hear. I decry the continents for their
careless drift. I detest the tectonic plates
for their indifferent quake. I wake up in
love with the ocean & fall asleep despising
all it has put between us. Perhaps if the
continents had never shaken themselves
free of one another we might find
ourselves disabused of this apathy. Perhaps
if we could hear the bomb dropping,
we might imagine what would happen
if it struck our own home. I am nostalgic
for a proximity that may not have mattered.
I find myself loathing a miracle.

MAGGIE SMITH

The Parable of the Bear

Beloveds, I keep picturing it
this way: we're standing, all of us,

between the Bear and every creature
the Bear calls prey, and half of us

step aside. Half of us aren't enough
to hold the Bear. It lumbers,

then, in a blur of claws and mange,
charges through. What did you think

would happen? The Bear would lose
its appetite? The Bear might be tamed

with a tiny bicycle, a propeller hat,
a gold sphere to balance on its nose?

I don't need to describe what happens
next: the smell of blood, the surprise

of white femur. Ones I have called
beloved, I keep picturing you

this way: sitting off to one side,
watching the Bear work, waiting to see

if it leaves any meat on the bones.

What I Carried

I carried my fear of the world
to my children, but they refused it.

I carried my fear of the world
on my chest, where I once carried
my children, where some nights it slept
as newborns sleep, where it purred
but mostly growled, where it licked
sweat from my clavicles.

I carried my fear of the world
and apprenticed myself to the fear.

I carried my fear of the world
and it became my teacher.
I carried it, and it repaid me
by teaching me how to carry it.

I carried my fear of the world
the way an animal carries a kill in its jaws
but in reverse: I was the kill, the gift.
Whose feet would I be left at?

I carried my fear of the world
as if it could protect me from the world.

I carried my fear of the world
and for my children modeled marveling
at its beauty but keeping my hands still—
keeping my eyes on its mouth, its teeth.

I carried my fear of the world.
I stroked it or I did not dare to stroke it.

I carried my fear of the world
and it became my teacher.
It taught me how to keep quiet and still

I carried my fear of the world
and my love for the world.
I carried my terrible awe.

I carried my fear of the world
without knowing how to set it down.

I carried my fear of the world
and let it nuzzle close to me,
and when it nipped, when it bit
down hard to taste me, part of me
shined: I had been right.

I carried my fear of the world
and it taught me I had been right.
I carried it and loved it
for making me right.

I carried my fear of the world
and it taught me how to carry it.

I carried my fear of the world
to my children and laid it down
at their feet, a kill, a gift.
Or I was laid down at their feet.

PATRICIA SMITH

Practice Standing Unleashed and Clean

Upon their arrival in America, more than twelve million immigrants were processed through the Ellis Island Immigration Center. Those who had traveled in second or third class were immediately given a thirty-second health inspection to determine if they were fit to enter their new country. A chalk checkmark on their clothing signaled a health problem and meant a stay in the Ellis Island Immigrant Hospital, where they either recovered or, if deemed incurable, were kept until they could be sent back home. Even if just one family member was sick, that person's entire family was turned away.

Hide the awkward jolt of jawline, the fluttering eye, that wide
brazen slash of boat-burned skin. Count each breath in order
to pacify the bloodless roiling just beneath the rib, to squelch
the mushrooming boom of tumor. Give fever another name.
I open my mouth, just to moan, but instead cluttered nouns,
so unAmerican, spew from my throat and become steam
in the room. That heat ripples through the meandering queue
of souls and someone who was once my uncle grows dizzy
with not looking at me. I am asked to temporarily unbutton
the clawing children from my heavy skirt, to pull the rough
linen blouse over my head and through my thick salted hair.
A last shelter thuds hard, pools around my feet on the floor.

I traveled with a whole chattering country's restless mass
weakening my shoulders. But I offer it as both yesterday
and muscle. I come to you America, scrubbed almost clean,
but infected with memory and the bellow of broiling spices
in a long-ago kitchen. I come with a sickness insistent upon
root in my body, a sickness that may just be a frantic twist
from one life's air to another. I ask for nothing but a home
with windows of circled arms, for a warm that overwhelms
the tangled sounds that say my name. I ask for the beaten
woman with her torch uplifted to find me here and loose
my new face of venom and virus. I have practiced standing
unleashed and clean. I have practiced the words I know.

So I pray this new country receive me, stark naked now,
forearms chapped raw, although I am ill in underneath ways.
I know that I am freakish, wildly fragrant, curious land. I stink
of seawater and the oversea moonwash I conjured to restart
and restart my migrant heart. All I can be is here, stretched
between solace and surrender, terrified of the dusty mark
that identifies me as poison in every one of the wrong ways.
I could perish here on the edge of everything. Or the chalk
mark could be a wing on my breastbone, unleashing me
in the direction of light. Someone will help me find my clothes
and brush the salt from my hair. I am marked perfect, and
I hear the word *heal* in a voice I thought I brought from home.

that's my

*son collapsed there my son crumpled there my son lying there my son
positioned there my daughter re-positioned there my daughter as exhibit a
there my daughter dumped over there my son hidden away there my son
colored blue there my son dangling there my son caged there my daughter on
the gurney there on the slab there in the drawer there my daughter splayed
there my son locked down there my son hanging there my son bleeding out
there my son growing frigid there my daughter deposited there my daughter
inside the chalk there my daughter being bagged there my son on the slab
there my son crushed there my son rearranged there my son crumpled in the
door there my daughter's neck shrinking in the noose there my daughter's
left eye over there my son as exhibit b there my son behind the wheel there my
son under the wheels there my son slumped over the wheel there my son my
daughter blooded and not moving in the doorway on the stoop down the
block in front of her kids just inside the barbershop face down in the street
outside the bodega inside the bodega in the alley behind the bodega on the
videotape a block from home just leaving home at home in the schoolyard
on the blacktop in his bed in her kitchen in my arms in my arms in my
arms that's my son shot to look thuggish that's my daughter shot to look
more animal shot as kill shot as prey shot as conquest shot as solution shot
as lesson shot as warning shot as comeback shot as payback shot for sport
shot for history that's my son not being alive any more there that's my child
coming to rest one layer below the surface of
the rest of my life*
                    there

CHRISTIAN TERESI

Nina Simone Explains Delusions to John Roberts

> "What unique perspective does a minority student bring to a
> physics class?"
>> —Chief Justice John Roberts, U.S. Supreme Court,
>> Fisher v. Texas, December 9, 2015

We were each once innocent—without the protection
Of our lies. Without dragons that each time revealed

Incrementally celebrate the not really and never were.
What passed coolly over forgotten pools and river rock—

Fused between unnamed prairie and unknown delta—
Still stretches unbroken without proclamation. We called

For the dead dog because toddlers do not understand death.
When Cortés arrived off the coast of Mexico he ordered

A native brought to his ship, as he believed was the right
Of the conquistador. He asked his captive. *Ma c'uhah than,*

The man replied, and the Spanish first heard Yucatán, the place
Of their discovery, where *Ma c'uhah than* in Mayan means,

"I do not understand you." Your vaudeville love for conquerors
Is only a lifeboat space between elbows. It goes away alive

And returns a falsetto. I'd like to introduce these songs
To boys from my youth who taunt and boast towards trinkets

They believe must be taken from their sister's room
And busted inside out by boredom and boot heels if only

To force confessions from their captives' throats. They are all
Protected by pretend. I'd rather not speak than speak in scatterings

Of a future where managers forget they still wear the old hats.
Be ancient, a forgotten language satisfied with being lost.

Nobody Explains Political Myopia to the Unrepentant Voter

Then neighbors wake to struggle out the faint sound
Of breaking glass, and children learn words that are hushed

To accept vanishing, and nobody figures the nightwatch
Forgot how to tell time. Then *history* atrophies into *story*,

Nobody says from the balcony, and fetching cake for nobody,
Are only acts that are an apology for what little is known

About the bottom where they reside. They are a perfume
Of climate and mud. They are nothing if not mad by fortune

That knows the hanged man is not always the bad sign.
They are joyously nobody in the same cosmos where

Some are paid to kick in doors and swarm warlike. Where
If a shortage of limes, and enough money to be made,

Then somebody will be killed over limes. There is no way
To depose the font where fear and greed are sourced

By ancient tumult. There is no way. Accept to build your life
Like those medieval doors that are so narrow they could not

Be entered by enemies in armor. Nobody comes close to well.

Etymology of the Ancient City

We labor to forget
The trees planted after strip-mining.

We forget we name them, *Tree
Of Heaven*, to help heal our excess.

We think it mercy to forge one narrative
By removing another. We plant heaven,

And feel blameless, but it is cruel. The trees
Also named ghetto palms in the field guides

For troubled things. Ghetto thought to be
From the Venetian *Ghet*, meaning waste or slag.

The place where they plant the unwanted.
Island where the Venetians forced them.

Island whose alluvium is washed by the discarded
They named ghetto, maybe from the Gothic

Gatwo, meaning street. The place they let live
By waste and whatever tangles grow

In the false distance. Close enough for work songs
Whose melody lingers when it arrives

As murmurs no longer fluent in their origin.
Living no further from their previous meaning

Than across a canal. In the small hours, impassable
Tides separate one into another. No longer

Concerned with what was said before. Ghetto
Cultivated possibly from the Hebrew *Get*,

Meaning a document allowing a wife other men
By forced separation. A divorce of the altogether,

Arrived at from the Sumerian, or Basque, or words
Lost by degrees imaginably as close to the language

Of heaven as ever permitted. In the voices
Of the ancient city, which is a variant of any city,

Night arrives from dusk when no one can tell
Between a wolf and a dog in the distance.

LEAH TIEGER

Electorate

The owl calls to itself its single question. The answer
has stray dog eyes. It says these men want to save us
in their image, tells us this woman serves existing power,
a necessary raincoat. There are so many more eggs to break.
The owl talks like an owl, the men like men. One talks
like Jesus. His gospel proceeds from one device to another,
our new minds a contagion, as much turned to him as to
his corn-haired Judas, a vote for the murder of reason,
a vote for the assassination of love. The owl is like him,
like us, which is to say we eat our own, our afterbirth
coins in the temple. They catch the light in green eyes
and soft, pale hands. This is how we tithe, by the white skin
of our teeth. There is a beginning no one can remember,
not even the owl, each feather a story of pomegranate
and flood. Each wing greets the air at our waking.
Each beat speaks the name of the almost nighttime woman
who lived without raincoats. She went without everything
there is to go without. At least there's this. These men
were never raised by pharaohs, adopted into power
with coal in their mouths. Oh how god speaks to them
and their tongues are burning leaves. They light the people
who hear them on fire, turn the black and white cities
that raised them into ash. Gray is not a meeting in the middle,
but the burnt remains of your home. There is an end
and no one knows it, not even the owl, who cradles its meal
in the cage of its feet. The owl brings us fur, brings us skeleton,
turns its hingeless head, and offers its only answer. You,
and you know how this goes. Those socialist Jews die bloody.
We will pray to them, ask them to save us. They're gone.

VINCENT TORO

The Savages

are right now double parked in front of the World Bank.
They ensconce their younglings in Hotchkiss. Berate the shampoo
girl at the salon. Indite travelogues for Condé Nast on their jaunt

to the Forest of Knives. The Savages put high tea on the company
card. Evade their co-pay for the ophthalmologist. Exit the fundraiser
for Parkinson's eight yoctoseconds after commencement of the blind

auction. The Savages are late for an engagement with their lifestyle
coach. They are in need of a social media director. Do consulting
on the side. Will take their grievance to the co-op board. Gouge

the damage for your grandmother's insulin. They raze low income
housing to make way for artisanal cheese. Gerrymander melanated
tribes into paralysis. The Savages wheedle city planners to reroute

toxic aqueducts away from their summer villas. They send memos
on official letterhead. Cite Foucault and de Beauvoir. Fabricate
market bubbles. Deny tenure. Moonlight with economic policy

institutes. The Savages cry during documentaries that epitomize
the anguish of the poor. They curate garment district exhibition
spaces. Acquire vineyards. Study abroad. They petrify themselves

at the perimeter of the dance floor. Accumulate interns. Note
that when they are presented with inadequate confection options
The Savages will commit acts of cannibalism without hesitation.

Should you encounter one in the wild, clutch your purse. Shield
your little ones. Pray you are engaging them during their cycle
of post-therapy contrition. If you see them advancing and there

is no shelter to take, play dead. In the event that you are bitten
by The Savages, do not attempt to call an emergency medical
technician. The Savages have already paid them not to show.

LEAH UMANSKY

Sonnet II

The close and contained are underloved and dumbwitted
And so is the disharmony of life, the knowing of neither greatness nor
  light quelled by
The riding off into the canary-hued dawn. There is so much to grieve,
  but sit. Sit. Sit
Here, I can plan a thread of sage advice, of sparked joys, as per your
  request.
Are you a relatable type? Sure, and here's a small concession of honesty.
  Would that interest
You? Good. Your passion can be blamed on what is comfortable or
  complacent, but lie
Still. *Exhale.* Decades ago, a brilliant means was pure fate, or poor
  misconduct, & everywhere
Everywhere, now, are halves of us, & halves of our sex. Our voices
  now cling
To the missives we send. Does this feel dismissive? Unrealistic?
  Mercurial? Insincere?
All of our halves are braided in a central tension, in a knot like
  childhood.
A brilliant way to end the suffering is with gravity. A mere lie down can
Solve all. And yes, you should interject more. Pull yourself to the
  center. Put
The day in loathing. Colonize what slugs, but breathe, you nice
  little thing,
Remember, you can stall, and hum and fray all you want.

this is a poem about survival

To be honest   the smallest hole of truth is a dungeon
It is disorienting.   I choose the choice I've made a thousand times

I want to say *bless,* but I mean *wild.*   I want to say *wild,*
but I mean, *bloody.*   The best place in the world is to be here
with me.

[this is a hell of a job being human]

There is so much to consider.   There is so much to satisfy.
There is so much to feel.   I can close myself like a fish,
hook-lipped and thin, bloody my mouth with metal, all to regard
the calm of the sea,   the sea.

See the barreling of my want

I Leave

a house of surrender. I finish my falling down.

I leave my certainties at the back:

my tea,
my book,
& my tv shows.

I clear the stiff dark fears away,
but they are alive.

Torched.

Aglow.

I can see the beauty fear can hold:
its control:

hypnosis

& stare.

It has an afterstrain.
A temperature that I must   cool   to.

I try to   shift   my thoughts.

This is remembering.

There is a pacing in all of us,
a climate of   *do's*   and   *do not's*.

You, *you inside,* your despair is too swift.
Your anguish is too early,
or too late.

It doesn't matter.

This is a new fate
& it will not always be
so hard.

It will not always be
so full
& bloodied.

At the cusp of the rising,
I can imagine the not-fear.
I can imagine the not-horror.

The suffering that ladders
                    through
                         me.

I am just one holder of a history.
I must stay calm.

        You, too, must stay calm.

Be it late or early,
you are fraught with thorns
            & brambles.

Stop.

We cannot feed
or strangle
what is predatory.

We can
clip their claws
& tame their madness into fatigue,

                    into the dank,

                         into the marrowed.

EMILY VOGEL

Orphan Leaves

Abrupt winter, late November, gold leaves
like grief-stricken orphans in the snow,
like twitterpated heartbeats
among random reveries of spring,
too far in their futurity to fathom.
What will blight us in this new age?
The glad illness
in the drenched air of April,
undercurrent of love in the loins,
a public lynching, perhaps
a thousand deportations?
The towering of an egregious
and oppressive enterprise?
Some animal ate the face
off of our month-old jack-o-lantern.
Some figure-head threatens
to eat the faces
of our very trembling humanity.
March, or walk softly,
carrying some big stick: jilted
yellow leaves, come for your
holiday donation of food. Snow,
fall and fall, like the dark and cascading hair
of the Virgin Mother, fall,
like the cold tears of whatever God
is blessing or distraction,
fall on the good and evil alike.
Come like holy blood, fall
on the absurdity of this tyranny:
redeem or destroy us,
as we might expect, as it goes,
as is the sharp and throbbing
jugular of history.

The New Elected "God"

Listen studiously. The deer are moving,
a near-blind traversal. So quiescent,
and yet the undertow of winter's silent prologue
is stirring like something clamorous.
No din, and yet the dead are groaning.
We cannot hear them, but we sense them,
and the snow falls—stark contrast
to the dimming evening. Listen,
like some sort of assiduous monk.
Nothing you can think of saying
will change the mercy killing
that is December, the small lights
that dot the air, so famished for joy
in the ghostly gunshot of new battle.
The faces: downcast, and so afraid,
that they all proceed as usual,
just as the fires of dissent are blazing.

JOE WEIL

Poem in Which I Shit on Unity

I don't want to come together.
I don't even agree with myself.
There's parts of me
even now, in Outer Mongolia
cursing over a cup of Kumis
and other parts riding the
back of a neutrino through
the center of a Trump sign.
I pass like a ghost through Latvia.
I am an Embryo curled
in the womb of a hot house Tulip.
There are those who want me
born so they can shoot me
legally later—(when I deserve it).
I am frost. I am fire and all four
winds pulling at the plastic strip
of this crime scene. I am told
today about a poem in which
three pissed off plant workers
in Michigan beat a Chinese man
to death, thinking him Japanese.
This was long ago, when Toyota
was kicking America's ass. I
wonder if they said: "Oops"
or "close enough." I wonder if
the moon is the same for
everyone just after, and nothing,
nothing, tilts or falls in grief
from the sky.

Red Land (A Satire in the Old Irish Poetic Sense)

I see red everywhere, though I'm losing my hair,
and I hate it, it's boring and sad
where the fair becomes foul and the foul becomes fair
and a nation goes stark raving mad.
It's red in all branches, the rich on their ranches
are branding, and Godly, and charmed
and pretending to be, just plain folks, don't you see.
they're the salt of the earth? (and well-armed).
Burn all the books, save the guns, and the looks
of the women. As trophies they count.
All the girls must line up from the A to D cup
to see if they're worthy to mount.
Oh give me a home where the buffalo roam
passed the frackers, and hackers, and hacks,
and no matter who's in—his executive's grin
will fall upon old Goldman Sachs.
Yes the God fearing bankers shall suffer no cankers
from mixing with green backs and gays.
And the Christian shall wave in the home of the brave
as he sings to his lord all due praise.
But if this is so, this medicine show,
this conning, this lying, this spew,
then I'd rather be dead in the land of all red
where only God's heaven is blue.

Early Winter (The Day After)

From the half-rotten ash-tree's topmost twig,
a mottled cloud dives—and all the ash keys quiver,
while out a little further, a murmuration
rises and falls upon the freezing river.
I join my own reflection to the geese
whose victory v moves from the rivers sedge
and skyward, a broken circle of rosary beads
vanishes. A blue jay takes the pledge
of his own name. Such a wild crested bird
must have a reason to the riot in his rhyme:
and then I see the red-tailed hawk that rides
on thermals, wings spread, how peacefully it glides
then drops—a thousand feet to snatch a hare.
I bite my lip and bleed into its cry.

JAMEKA WILLIAMS

[my heroes lie in boxes]

my heroes lie in boxes
television sets and prison cells

grandma's girlhood picture shows
enjoyed cowboys and confederates

white with drunken twang and limp
smiting indians, a nigger or two

jailed them in boxes no bigger
than a game of solitaire

with pissy mattresses stained ochre
so nostalgic, acrid, hot

those boys dreamed they'd slept
all this time on their mamas' clay lawns

remembered reels of those cowboys
pinching their grandfathers for skin games

locked Peacemakers inside jaws, brown faces
swollen to the shape of an infant's hunger

a testifier, his color subtle as a stone,
with hungry eyes, instead flees out of frame

my heroes don't know any better, so
they clipped the sheriff

and gave their sons a cool, sleek hate
whose whistle runs deep, is black

its shape thick as the cradle
of a gun's chamber

Thoughts on a Birthday Party

Atlanta: 1864, 2015

we celebrate because we are afraid

on this anniversary our child opened
his eyes to the disquieted morning

took his place in our fathers' Rage

They say we're always seeing rivers
of blood where there's only tangled

ribbons snagged under the racing
sneakers of our nephews

but Their truck beds: the Stars & Bars beats
the wind, saluting us over & over & over &

an early Christmas present, a token of Their
War, a son's birthday wish

if we saw an intent muzzle or length of rope

we must have imagined it

They say we always have two loaded
fingers pressed against our jugular veins

Asks: aren't you proud to have bodies
that are burning, but not on fire

For the Love of God

you have lived so many years
but tell me have you un-lived

did not rise with the sun & the Blackness
which soaks our skin devastated you

weighed you down deep into the depths
of your mattress comforter

damned   eyes   they have not
seen the glory only a hell quieter

the sound of our voices breaks to a shrill
tinnitus   "please," you say, "you'll

injure the public with your presence alone"
open your body   how white you are

inside: egg & bones
how un-living you are

"leave your disease at home"
"you are not a thin Blackness"

but they have ways of thinning us out
a sigh escapes our tarred lungs

& we tremble with our sorrow's rebellion
but you just look to the sky:

"does the rain have a white father"
"from who's womb comes the ice"

Black, or I Sit on My Front Porch in the Projects Waiting for God

& when she arrived she did not disappoint. Her low-hanging breasts, the nipples puffy & down-turned. The smile of gapped teeth, fed with coconut oil & a side of fried okra. She petted my wooly head, ran her swollen knuckles down my bitter spine & recoiled. Cursed the weight of my sorrow with hymn-song. Why is there no milk or honey in you, child? God asked & I said: I burn I cry What's new. God scoffed: how many wars did Helen fuel with her labia, her will? She asked & answered: exactly the number she needed to win men to their deaths. I interrogated: does God have a pussy where her soul should be? I keep it in a vanity box, she said, with my menopause & my pocket change & my wit. Then suddenly I remembered being a girl of ten climbing the stairs of my grandmother's house on Potter Street. In her bedroom, I cracked the spine of her jewelry box studded with broken sequins like baby's teeth & I clasped her pearl earrings, her needles & threads, her shards of glass in between my hands for supplication & declared that I had just held a woman like a man should. Then God placed my hands on her face & I fingered the wrinkles across her eyebrows & down her cheeks & she said that that was Woman & then I rubbed the pouch in which her children drowned & she said that that was Woman also & she unveiled a torn hymen & declared that that was Woman too & she placed a hand inside the lacunae where my heart should be & said I was Woman too. & who says God is cruel & without color?

PHILLIP B. WILLIAMS

from **Interruptive**

What can I do but make of the eyes of others
my own eyes, but make of the world a ghazal
whose radif is a haunting of *me, me, me?*

Somewhere there are fingers still whole
to tell the story of the empire that devours fingers.
Somewhere there is a city where even larvae

cannot clean the wounds of the living
and cannot eat on the countless dead
who are made to die tomorrow and tomorrow.

Carrion beetles and boot bottoms grind corpses
powder-soft to feed the small-mouthed gods
of gardens and wind. Roses made to toss their silk

to earth like immolated gowns, hills
spewing ribbons of charred air from cities
occupied by artillery and pilfered grain, limbs

blown from their bodies and made into an alphabet
that builds this fool song, even now, presented
before you as false curative, as vacant kiss — even

what is lost in the fabrication of strangers needs naught
from strangers. Even *somewhere* stings with stillness,
stings with a home not surrendered but a given.

•

But I have not been with my feet on the earth
there where bullets make use of skin like flags
make use of the land. My thinking is as skeletal

as the bombed-out schools and houses
untelevised. What do I know of occupation
but my own colonized thinking to shake

free from. While my days themselves tremble
from time and shake off place to feel falsely
placeless, a hollow empathy as if its soft chisel

could make of this wall—my ignorance mighty
before me upon which drawn figures alight
against the stone—my own; what is mine is

the wall my votes and non-votes, my purchases
wrapped in unthought have built and stretched,
undead gray. There are no secrets in debris.

I have a home I hate, its steel and lights
red and blue upon me. Home itself a mist
through which I pass and barely notice.

Home, to assume you are home is to assume
I am welcome in you—to what degree let the wounds
say so—and can come and go as I please.

The television tells me *Over there*, and one must point
with a fully extended arm to show how far from,
how unlike here *there* really is. *Over there*

where they blow each other up over land and God.
And it feels good to stretch as if from waking—
this silence could be called a kind of sleep—and think

beyond, where I am not and where those who are
are not—wall upon which drawings of fists
strike skyward and faces of activists stare into me

from my Google search. Turnstiles separate
home from home. Barbed wire catches clouds
in its coil saws. What do I know of injustice

but having a home throughout which bullets,
ballots, and brutality trifecta against
people who were here before here was here

and people were brought here to change
the landscape of *humanity*? That word has rolling hills
and towering walls. To hammer against it not to get

to the other side — believe nothing is there —
but to make obsolete *side* — know there is nothing.
I know this: my metaphors have small arms,

my wallet has made monstrous my reflection,
I have done terrible things by being alive.
I have built a wonder of terror with my life.

•

8 Meters {

wall wall wall wall wall wall wall
wall wall wall wall wall wall wall
wall wall wall wall wall wall wall
wall wall wall wall wall wall wall
wall wall wall wall wall wall wall
wall wall wall wall wall wall wall
wall wall wall wall wall wall wall
wall wall child wall wall wall wall

[Image of an eight-meter-tall wall, constructed by connected
prefabrications. Interspersed among them are surveillances (I'll make
them pay). What is closed opens then settles. Spill: a scream, what makes
it. On the wall a body leans, which is a caption: "This is not prayer."
(Which side are you on?) Here where there is no here, endurance
measured by a field's disruption and around it what makes possible a
furthering (to settle this in court or to settle in this courtyard). Argument:
this thinking is real because it has been made touchable if touch is the
mutual rejection of objects from entering into the other (let's settle this

once and for all) who's going to pay for what reaches toward and fails at
heaven? To settle the debt, settle in silence. If it is not silent (this roaring
(is it fire / stone / a pen lifting (ban no ban no b—) or falling?) is it
home?) make it so.]

•

Between his war with self and the war
in a sand-sealed country neither of us could spell,
juvie took from R what little childhood

Chicago hadn't taken. Between bloody showers
and rushed meals, him forced by bigger boys
until pain became expectation and expectation

pleasure. A shortened sentence meant fighting
for a country against people for whom R held
no hatred while hating the ones he fought for.

There is venom in coercion misnamed loyalty.
Boys and bloody water in his head when he left
to fight in heat and camo. Then in the barrack's

shower, three soldiers raped R. Sand is the Plaza
of Pardon. Wind draws its name across the grains
and leaves the grains with the name it gave.

Who would I be after so many tried to live
in me forcibly? R in the desert, our Skype
lost connection when an explosion blew out

what little service he had. *Oh shit,*
we been hit. Then blackout silence
and my pulse explicit. Let us rejoice in this:

war is a love song that makes your body dangerous
to others, that makes you unlivable. You become more
private. You are always early to yourself.

When I saw him again, marijuana discharged him
dishonorably and the men inside him shooting guns
and shooting cum went with him. This is one veteran's

legacy, one man I know and have lost to distance,
my own pulling me from everything I'm meant to
hold close. What do I know of exile but self-imposed

self-removal. When R kissed my forehead goodbye
the first time I felt citizenly, patriotic, my white
handkerchief au revoir-ing a friend from my mind

who returned with sand hissing down his pant legs.
A hero is an hourglass. For what
does his countdown drop its grains, skull to heel?

●

One night, words came, swift
as if prayed for, showing
myself to me to correct myself:

Grief unhides beneath bombed mosques
while the sky blows into pale blue absence
dust and vaporized skin.

Grief and sky, unrequited lovers. Whose hurt
could hold the other's? Grief knows the passage
of the worm and the temperatures of dirt.

Sky knows the neon of kite sail and tail.
Fifteen thousand names written in the air
by ribbon, rhombi billowed into shields,

glide into the Guinness Book of Records, *memories*
passed page to page across oceans and treaties
in ink out-blacking smoke. Waves leave soft creases

on the Gaza Strip and know airborne diamonds
by the shadows of their measured shapes
tethered like falcons to a child's quick hands...

How to mistake American arrogance for love,
to think kites could humanize the already-human
and hide the anti-human from its history.

Why cloak our custom of cloaking? To make
palatable the blade we turn on ourselves we turn it
on others. In good light the metal will give

us back to ourselves. Does the wolf know
it has a reflection? Ask the water if it shows
to us its beast self or has one given to it.

•

[Image of an eight-meter-tall wall, over which is painted "Is you coming or going or is I?" A ray of light ballistic through the form is both answer and rejection of an answer's possibility.]

•

Tragedy disturbs tragedy.
There can never be just one
way to see the end to ourselves.

The Mediterranean has endless room
where capsized boats of hundreds bloomed
once with refugees. Water can't be trusted.

The wind with its countless hands hasting
water into waves can't be seen so can't be
trusted even though we feel it, even when we

know along its unseen force bobs curt hymns
from the dead to the living. We don't hear them
rising from the salt like fins. We hear bombs

and think *Each storm carries the broken cries
of a broken nation in its contortion.* Alibi
for the living is the land: it's the earth

itself that refuses the dead a home in burr
or field, in the stone plateaus or tableaux
of scree from a city of wild boars and roads

that lead to a burning garden, a gutted church,
a school uniform hemmed by soldiers, a birch
limned with blood and pointing dually

west to a row of houses roofless but for crows and east
to a rifle hung above a threshold like a saint.
Something's always watching, well-aimed

and unkind, empty and on fire or just-
finished burning. And the water will rust
the skin, will extinguish the fire and the flesh.

Baptism is what the living do. The rest
are left to idols of fish and worm, are left
with the living's pens and books bereft

and intricate as mausolea woven from husks
of stories the dead cannot tell. They brux
in our renditions as we cull their truth for our song.

•

The wilderness within us creeps closer
to the surface of thought and burial.
We drag ourselves from the selves

that laid bear traps that trapped us into our own
dragging, one leg limp behind like a memory
pain brings forward. Low grass collects

pockets of our blood as if any gloss
could reduce droughts in the smallest needs.
If we make eye contact with the most beleaguered

of us, we pray the remains of god would shower
spears to smite clean such embarrassment. We are not
neighbors, just near. We are failures of nature

and the stars burn down through trees no light
we can trust. Because we were shrewd with conviction
the pads of our right hands' digits have singed

into them one letter each to spell *faith*. What we touch
with that hand will fell our enemies
who are ourselves. We draw a maze with our blood,

follow paths drawn from the cruelties sculpted
into another's body. I am losted by a child's missing eye,
dead-ended by a family encrusted with shrapnel.

If I follow my own disaster more closely,
if I allow buzzards spiraling above prophecy
enough to reveal time as caught in the loop

of their pinions, if I remove my shirt
from my bloodied torso and twist
from it my own oil, if in my pocket

I find the final ballot before the mine
was tripped in god's patience, if I see my vote
had predicted the immolation of seasons

and the beheading of goats sacrificed to rain
that washed away no blood and emulsified
sickness into the oceans and seas, if pain rises

from the mouths of the dead in the shape
the dead took when alive, if all this time
we've been building tombs and calling them home—

•

[Image of an eight-meter-tall wall bearing a hole in its center, or a
1.7272-meter-tall wall, which is me, bearing a hole in my center. I am the
wall and the hole is what makes me better. I want to be better.]

•

Hajjar, does a body on its back act as the body's own
grief? Is a body downed the mind's shadow? If we must love
our souls, does that mean we must love what leaves?

JANE WONG

The Act of Killing

It is early and I have no one to trust.
The sun wrestles wildly about me,
throwing light in unbearable places.
Each day, I wear this necklace of flares,
bright kicks against the throat. Each day,
the earth wobbles in its orbit. I am
in the process of creating an army.
A hive mind, honeyed in the eyes and
pure in purpose. Wasps drone among
roses I stole from my grandfather's
headstone. Drones watch as my father
kills a man over a bad bet. He presses
the man's head down into a floor flooded
with enough bills to build a country.
Covered in warm towels, my father drones
in his sleep. He sends a telegram to me:
I could have been a mathematician.
Equal signs multiply across state lines,
dividers of the familiar. Surveillance works
like this: *stop*. Intentions drag through
the mud, daily. The spoiled sun runs
its yolk. I run my mouth all over town.
All around me, the grievance tree weeps
with wasps. For, what is a bullet without
an arm to go through? I cross and cradle
my arms. When the sun goes down,
I check my eyes to see if they are still there.

Spoiled

To tell the truth, I have forgotten
which year goes with what.

My memory: as good as milk.
My family: spoiled through

and through. Pure as mold
on a September nectarine,

we refuse to announce defeat,
death. In this house, the margins

of mourning are tucked in,
pleated to the neck.

In August, my uncle dies
and no one tells his children.

He crosses his arms
in a blue suit in a coffin

where the ants
want in. In December,

my brother and I bundle up
for a storm that goes

through another town.
What were we preparing for?

My mother warns us:
beware of well-lit places.

Beware of fires burning
in the dark. If there is a spider

under your cup,
what will you do about it?

JAVIER ZAMORA

Looking at a Coyote

among thirty dusty men the only wet thing

　　　　　　　　　　the mouth of the coyote

is a mini zoo we are from many countries

　　　　　　　　　　in which there are many coyotes

500 bucks and we're off think about it

　　　　　　　　　　is the shortest verse of a corrido

a gila monster and a coyote are one

　　　　　　　　　　a gila monster and a coyote *and* a gringo are one

strewn bottles melt dirt

　　　　　　　　　　the coyote's tongue fills them

we don't know which to swat the coyote or the froth

　　　　　　　　　　the mosquitoes or the flies

gringos why do you see us illegal don't you think

　　　　　　　　　　we are the workers around you

we speak different accents yours included and we know

　　　　　　　　　　también the coyote is suspect of what we say

when the coyote hears helicopters

　　　　　　　　　　in Nike shoes he trots Arizona

Nogales whores close their doors

　　　　　　　　　　the coyote trots Arizona in Nike shoes

the desert is still the coyote must be tired

　　　　　　　　　　in his shadow he sees searchlights

it's day all night it's dusting and it's going to dust

　　　　　　　　　　the coyote rests under yuccas

Second Attempt Crossing

for Chino

In the middle of that desert that didn't look like sand
        and sand only,
in the middle of those acacias, whiptails, and coyotes, someone yelled
        "¡La Migra!" and everyone ran.
In that dried creek where 40 of us slept, we turned to each other
        and you flew from my side in the dirt.

Black-throated sparrows and dawn
        hitting the tops of mesquites,
beautifully. Against the herd of legs,

        you sprinted back toward me,
I jumped on your shoulders,
        and we ran from the white trucks. It was then the gun
ready to press its index.

        I said, "freeze, Chino, ¡pará por favor!"

So I wouldn't touch their legs that kicked you,
        you pushed me under your chest,
and I've never thanked you.

        Beautiful *Chino*—

the only name I know to call you by—
        farewell your tattooed chest:
the M, the S, the 13. Farewell
        the phone number you gave me
when you went east to Virginia,
        and I went west to San Francisco.

You called twice a month,
        then your cousin said the gang you ran from
in San Salvador
        found you in Alexandria. Farewell
your brown arms that shielded me then,
        that shield me now, from La Migra.

Acknowledgements

All of the poems in this anthology appear with permission from their authors and with gratitude to the following journals and presses:

Hanif Abdurraqib, "It's Just That I'm Not Really Into Politics": *BOAAT*; "& who, this time": *The Rumpus*; "I Don't Know Any Longer Why the Flags Are at Half-Staff": *Split This Rock*

Kaveh Akbar, "Unburnable the Cold is Flooding Our Lives": *TriQuarterly*; "Despite My Efforts Even My Prayers Have Turned into Threats": *Poetry*

María Isabel Alvarez, "In America": *DIALOGIST*

Eloisa Amezcua, "When Mexico Sends Its People, They're Not Sending Their Best": *Literary Hub*; "Elegy": *Assaracus*

Nin Andrews, "Why I am Not an Orgasm": *Plume*

William Archila, "This is for Henry": *The Art of Exile* (Bilingual Press, 2009); "The Line": *The Gravedigger's Archaeology* (Red Hen Press, 2015)

Fatimah Asghar, "If They Should Come for Us": *Poetry*

Chaun Ballard, "Pantoum": *Pittsburgh Poetry Review*; "The Necessity of Poetry": *International Poetry Review*

Zeina Hashem Beck, "the Days don't stop": *Rattle*

Bruce Bennett, "America in 2015" and "The Lake Isle of Anywhere": *The Donald Trump of the Republic* (FootHills Publishing, 2016)

Rosebud Ben-Oni, "And All the Songs We Are Meant To Be": *The Shallow Ends*

Brian Brodeur, "Lullaby for an Autocrat": *32 Poems.*

Joel Brouwer, "Some Varieties of Political Activism" from *Off Message* © 2016 by Joel Brouwer. Reprinted with permission of Four Way Books. All rights reserved.

Nickole Brown, "Inauguration Day, 2017": *Rise Up Review* and *Poets Speak (While We Still Can)*; "Trump's Tic Tacs": *Truth To Power: Writers Respond To The Rhetoric of Hate & Fear* and *If You Can Hear This: Poems in Protest of an American Inauguration* (Sibling Rivalry Press, 2017)

Tina Cane, "Avocado a la Ionesco": *Love's Executive Order*

Cortney Lamar Charleston, "Feeling Fucked Up" and "Chillary Clinton Said 'We Have to Bring Them to Heal'": *Rattle*; "Postmortem: 11/9/16": *DIALOGIST*

Kyle Dargan, "Americana" and "Mountebank": *The Rumpus*

Danielle Cadena Deulen, "American Curse," "On the Uncertainty of Our Judgment," and "We Are Bored": *Our Emotions Get Carried Away Beyond Us* (Barrow Street Press, 2015).

Natalie Diaz, "Post-Colonial Love Poem": *New Republic*.

Dante Di Stefano, "National Anthem with Elegy and Talon": *DIALOGIST*

celeste doaks, "American Herstory": *Split This Rock*

Martín Espada, "How We Could Have Lived or Died This Way" and "Isabel's Corrido": *Vivas to Those Who Have Failed* (W.W. Norton, 2016); "Sleeping on the Bus," "Jorge the Church Janitor Finally Quits," and "Alabanza: In Praise of Local 100": *Alabanza: New and Selected Poems 1982-2002* (W. W. Norton, 2003)

Joshua Jennifer Espinoza, "The Moon Is Trans," "[It is quiet in the morning.]," and "[The woman is about hair]": *The Feminist Wire*; "[It is quiet in the morning.]": *Electric Cereal*

Brian Fanelli, "Post-Election": *Popshot*

Ariel Francisco, "American Night, American Morning": *Origins Literary Review*

Tony Gloeggler, "On the Seventh Day": *Paterson Literary Review* and

Until the Last Light Leaves (NYQ Books, 2015)
Ruth Goring, "America, if": *Iron Horse Literary Review*

Sonia Greenfield, "Alternate Facts": *Anti-Heroin Chic*

David Hernandez, "All-American": *Dear, Sincerely* (University of Pittsburgh Press, 2016); "These Are Brave Days": *Rise Up Review*

Luther Hughes, "Self-Portrait as Crow": *Touched* (Sibling Rivalry Press, 2018)

Kenan Ince, "Sickle": *Black Heart Magazine*; "Mollusks" and "Trickle-Down Theory": *Permafrost*; "Resolution": *Rise Up Review*; "Ode to United Fruit": *Banango Street*

Maria Melendez Kelson, "El Villain": *Flexible Bones* (University of Arizona Press, 2010) and *The Best American Poetry Blog*

Dana Levin, "Winning": *Love's Executive Order*

Timothy Liu, "Protest Song": *Rattle*

Denise Low, "Andrew Jackson, I See You": *Yellow Medicine Review*

George Ella Lyon, "This Just In from Rancho Politico": *COUNTERPUNCH*

Shane McCrae, "Everything I Know About Blackness I Learned from Donald Trump": *Love's Executive Order*

Sjohnna McCray, "Portrait of My Father as a Young Black Man," "Burning Down Suburbia," and "Price Check": *Rapture* (Graywolf Press, 2016)

Erika Meitner, "I'll Remember You as You Were, Not as What You'll Become": *Love's Executive Order*

Rajiv Mohabir, "Inaugural Poem": *The Rumpus*

Kamilah Aisha Moon, "Notes on a Mass Stranding": *The Quarry*; "A Superwoman Chooses another Way to Fly" and "What James Craig

Anderson's Ghost Might Say (July 26, 2011)": *The Feminist Wire.*
"Notes on a Mass Stranding" and "A Superwoman Chooses Another
Way to Fly" from *She Has a Name* © 2013 by Kamilah Aisha Moon.
Reprinted with permission of Four Way Books. All rights reserved.

Abby E. Murray, "Poem for My Daughter Before the March": *Rattle
Online;* "My Daughter Asked for This": *Rise Up Review*

Susan Nguyen, "A list of directives": *Queen Mob's Teahouse*

Matthew Olzmann, "Despite the Kicking of Small Animals": *Love's
Executive Order*

Annette Oxindine, "Now That Spring Is Coming, More Decrees":
Rise Up Review

Gregory Pardlo, "For Which It Stands" and "Written By Himself"
from *Digest* © 2014 by Gregory Pardlo. Reprinted with permission
of Four Way Books. All rights reserved.

Craig Santos Perez, "Love Poem in the Time of Climate Change
(Sonnet XII & XVII)": *New Republic;* "Thanksgiving in the
Anthropocene, 2015": *Rattle*

Xandria Phillips, "–Bigly–": *Foundry;* "Elegy for the Living and
Breathing": *Reasons for Smoking;* and "She Makes Me Notice": *The
Pinch*

Kevin Prufer, "The Art of Fiction": *Copper Nickel;* "The Translator":
Paris Review; "The Mexicans": *Boulevard;* "Cruelties": *Kenyon Review.*
"National Anthem" from *National Anthem* © 2008 by Kevin Prufer.
Reprinted with permission of Four Way Books. All rights reserved.
"In a Beautiful Country" from *In a Beautiful Country* © 2011 by
Kevin Prufer. Reprinted with permission of Four Way Books. All
rights reserved.

Dean Rader, "America I Do Not Call Your Name Without Hope":
San Francisco Chronicle

Julian Randall, "The Search for Frank Ocean or a Brief History of
Disappearing": *Rattle*

Camille Rankine, "Aubade": *Poem-a-Day, Poets.org*
Alexandra Lytton Regalado, "La Mano": *Green Mountain Review* and *The Best American Poetry Blog*

Alison C. Rollins, "The Beastangel" and "Why Is We Americans": *Poetry*

Nicole Santalucia, "Thumping in Central Pennsylvania": *The Boiler*; "Supermarket Blowout": *Radar Poetry*

sam sax, "Doctrine": *Poem-a-Day, Poets.org*

Lauren Marie Schmidt. "In Defense of Poetry," "The Fourth of July," and "The Social Worker's Advice": *Filthy Labors* (Northwestern University Press, 2017)

Raena Shirali, "Dare I Write It": *Dusie*

Clint Smith, "Pangaea": *The Rumpus*

Maggie Smith, "The Parable of the Bear": *f(r)iction*; "What I Carried": *Redivider*

Patricia Smith, "Practice Standing Unleashed and Clean": *Poets.org*; "*that's my*": *The Normal School*

Christian Teresi, "Nina Simone Explains Delusions to John Roberts": *Narrative*

Leah Tieger, "Electorate": *Rattle*

Vincent Toro, "The Savages": *Love's Executive Order*

Leah Umansky, "Sonnet II": *Hermeneutic Chaos*; "this is a poem about survival": *Whiskey Island*

Phillip B. Williams, "*from* Interruptive": *Poetry*

Jane Wong, "The Act of Killing": *Tupelo Quarterly*; "Spoiled": *The Seattle Review of Books*

Javier Zamora, "Looking at a Coyote" and "Second Attempt Crossing": *Poetry*

Contributor Notes

HANIF ABDURRAQIB is a poet, essayist, and cultural critic from Columbus, Ohio. His first collection of poems, *The Crown Ain't Worth Much,* was released by Button Poetry in 2016. His first collection of essays, *They Can't Kill Us Until They Kill Us,* is forthcoming from Two Dollar Radio in winter 2017.

KAVEH AKBAR's poems appear recently or soon in *The New Yorker, Poetry, Tin House, Ploughshares, FIELD, Georgia Review, PBS NewsHour, Harvard Review, American Poetry Review, Narrative, The Poetry Review, AGNI, New England Review, Prairie Schooner, Virginia Quarterly Review, Best New Poets 2016, Guernica, Boston Review,* and elsewhere. His debut full-length collection, *Calling a Wolf a Wolf,* is forthcoming with Alice James Books in Fall 2017, and his chapbook, *Portrait of the Alcoholic,* is out with Sibling Rivalry Press. The recipient of a 2016 Ruth Lilly and Dorothy Sargent Rosenberg Fellowship from the Poetry Foundation and the Lucille Medwick Memorial Award from the Poetry Society of America, Kaveh was born in Tehran, Iran, and currently lives and teaches in Florida.

MARÍA ISABEL ALVAREZ received her MFA in fiction from Arizona State University. Her short stories have appeared in *Black Warrior Review, Sonora Review, Gulf Coast, Arts & Letters,* and *Puerto del Sol,* among other venues, and her poetry has been published in *DIALOGIST, Rust + Moth, Breakwater Review,* and *Glass: A Journal of Poetry.*

ELOISA AMEZCUA's debut collection, *From the Inside Quietly,* is the inaugural winner of the Shelterbelt Poetry Prize, selected by Ada Limón, forthcoming from Shelterbelt Press. She is the author of three chapbooks: *On Not Screaming* (Horse Less Press, 2016) *Symptoms of Teething,* winner of the 2016 Vella Chapbook Award (Paper Nautilus Press, 2017), and *Mexicamericana* (Porkbelly Press, 2017). She currently lives in Phoenix and is founder and editor-in-chief of *The Shallow Ends: A Journal of Poetry.*

NIN ANDREWS' poems have appeared in many literary journals and anthologies including *Ploughshares, Agni, The Paris Review,* and four editions of *Best American Poetry.* The author of 6 chapbooks and 6 full-length poetry collections, she has won two Ohio individual artist grants, the Pearl Chapbook Contest, the Kent State University chapbook contest, and the Gerald Cable Poetry Award. She is also the editor of a book of translations of the Belgian poet, Henri Michaux, *Someone Wants to Steal My Name.* Her book, *Why God Is a Woman,* was published by BOA Editions in 2015.

Poet and teacher **WILLIAM ARCHILA** earned his MFA in poetry from the University of Oregon, where he was given the Fighting Fund Fellow Award. His first collection of poetry, *The Art of Exile* (Bilingual Review Press, 2009) won an International Latino Book Award in 2010, an Emerging Writer Fellowship Award from the Writer's Center in Bethesda, MD, and was selected for The Fifth Annual Debut Poets Round Up in Poets & Writers. His second book, *The Gravedigger's Archaeology* (Red Hen Press), won the 2013 Letras Latinas/Red Hen Poetry Prize and was also featured in Poets & Writers' Page One. He has been published in *American Poetry Review, The Georgia Review, AGNI, Notre Dame Review,* and *Copper Nickle,* and the anthologies *Theatre Under My Skin: Contemporary Salvadoran Poetry, Wide Awake Poets of Los Angeles and Beyond,* and *The Wandering Song: Central American Writing in the United States.* He also has poems forthcoming in *Prairie Schooner* and *Los Angeles Review of Books*

FATIMAH ASGHAR is a Pakistani, Kashmiri, Muslim American writer. She is the author of the chapbook *After* (YesYes Books, 2015), the collection *If They Come For Us* (Oneworld, 2018) and the writer and co-creator of the Emmy-nominated web series *Brown Girls.* She is a member of the Dark Noise Collective and a 2017 recipient of the Ruth Lilly and Dorothy Sargent Rosenberg Poetry Fellowship from the Poetry Foundation.

CHAUN BALLARD was raised in both St. Louis, Missouri, and San Bernardino, California. For seven years now, he and his wife have been teaching in the Middle East and West Africa. He holds an MFA from the University of Alaska, Anchorage. He's had poems recently published by *Columbia Poetry Review, HEArt Online, Pittsburgh Poetry Review, Rattle, The Caribbean Writer,* and other literary magazines.

ZEINA HASHEM BECK is a Lebanese poet. Her most recent collection, *Louder than Hearts,* won the 2016 May Sarton New Hampshire Poetry Prize. She's also the author of two chapbooks: *3arabi Song,* winner of the 2016 Rattle Chapbook Prize, and *There*

Was and How Much There Was, a 2016 smith|doorstop Laureate's Choice, selected by Carol Ann Duffy. Her first collection, *To Live in Autumn,* won the 2013 Backwaters Prize. Her work has won Best of the Net, has been nominated for the Pushcart Prize and the Forward Prize, and has appeared in *Ploughshares, Poetry, Poetry Northwest, Ambit,* and *The Rialto,* among others. She lives in Dubai, where she has founded and runs PUNCH, a poetry and open mic collective. She reads in the Middle East and internationally.

BRUCE BENNETT was born in Philadelphia, Pennsylvania, in 1940. He received a BA, MA, and PhD from Harvard University. Bennett is the author of 10 books of poetry, including *Just Another Day in Just Our Town: Poems New and Selected 2000-2016* (Orchises Press, 2017), *Something Like Karma* (Clandestine Press, 2009), Subway Figure (Orchises Press, 2009), and *Navigating the Distances: Poems New and Selected* (Orchises Press, 1999). From 1967 to 1970, Bennett taught at Oberlin College, where he cofounded and edited *Field: Contemporary Poetry and Poetics.* He then went on to cofound and edit *Ploughshares.* In 1973, he began teaching at Wells College, where he served as Director of the creative writing program and cofounded Wells College Press. He retired in 2014, and is now Professor Emeritus of English. He lives in Aurora, New York.

Born to a Mexican mother and Jewish father, **ROSEBUD BEN-ONI** is a recipient of the 2014 NYFA Fellowship in Poetry and a CantoMundo Fellow; her most recent collection of poems, *turn around, BRXGHT XYXS,* was selected as Agape Editions' EDITORS' CHOICE, and will be published in 2019. She is an Editorial Advisor for VIDA: Women in Literary Arts. Her work appears or is forthcoming in *POETRY, The American Poetry Review, Tin House, Black Warrior Review, TriQuarterly, Prairie Schooner, Arts & Letters,* among others; recently, her poem "Poet Wrestling with Angels in the Dark" was commissioned by the National September 11 Memorial & Museum in New York City. She writes weekly for *The Kenyon Review* blog, and teaches creative writing at UCLA Extension's Writers' Program.

Brian Brodeur is the author of the poetry collections *Natural Causes* (2012) and *Other Latitudes* (2008), as well as the poetry chapbooks *Local Fauna* (2015) and *So the Night Cannot Go on Without Us* (2007). New poems and essays appear in *American Poetry Review, The Hopkins Review, Measure, The Missouri Review, Pleiades,* and

The Writer's Chronicle. Founder and Coordinator of the Veterans Writing Workshop of Richmond, Indiana, he lives with his wife and daughter in the Whitewater River Valley.

Poet and critic **JOEL BROUWER** is the author of the collections *Exactly What Happened, Centuries, And So,* and *Off Message.* He has held fellowships from the National Endowment for the Arts, the Mrs. Giles Whiting Foundation, and the John Simon Guggenheim Foundation. He is chair of the Department of English at the University of Alabama.

NICKOLE BROWN received her MFA from the Vermont College, studied literature at Oxford University, and was the editorial assistant for the late Hunter S. Thompson. She worked at Sarabande Books for ten years. Her first collection, *Sister,* a novel-in-poems, was first published in 2007 by Red Hen Press and a new edition will be reissued by Sibling Rivalry Press in 2018. Her second book, a biography-in-poems called *Fanny Says,* came out from BOA Editions in 2015, and the audio book of that collection became available in 2017. She was an Assistant Professor at the University of Arkansas at Little Rock for four years until she gave up her beloved time in the classroom in hope of writing full time. Currently, she is the Editor for the Marie Alexander Poetry Series and teaches periodically at a number of places, including the Sewanee School of Letters MFA Program, the Great Smokies Writing Program at UNCA, and the Hindman Settlement School. She lives with her wife, poet Jessica Jacobs, in Asheville, NC, where she volunteers at a four different animal sanctuaries. Currently, she's at work on a bestiary of sorts about these animals, but it won't consist of the kind of pastorals that always made her (and most of the working-class folks she knows) feel shut out of nature and the writing about it— these poems speak in a queer, Southern-trash-talking kind of way about nature beautiful, but damaged and dangerous.

TINA CANE is the author of *Dear Elena: Letters for Elena Ferrante* (Skillman Avenue Press) *and Once More with Feeling* (Veliz Books). She currently serves as the Poet Laureate of Rhode Island.

CORTNEY LAMAR CHARLESTON is the author of *Telepathologies,* selected by D.A. Powell for the 2016 Saturnalia Books Poetry Prize. A recipient of fellowships from Cave Canem and The Conversation

Literary Festival, his poems have appeared in *Beloit Poetry Journal, Gulf Coast, The Iowa Review, The Journal, New England Review, POETRY, River Styx, TriQuarterly* and elsewhere.

JIM DANIELS' new book, *Birth Marks,* was published by BOA Editions in 2013. Other books published in 2011 include *Trigger Man: More Tales of the Motor City, Having a Little Talk with Capital P Poetry,* and *All of the Above.* In 2010, he wrote and produced the independent film "Mr. Pleasant," which appeared in many film festivals across the country. He also published *From Milltown to Malltown,* a collaboration with photographer Charlee Brodsky. His poem "Factory Love" is displayed on the roof of a race car. A native of Detroit, Daniels teaches at Carnegie Mellon University in Pittsburgh.

KYLE DARGAN was born in Newark, New Jersey. He earned his BA from the University of Virginia and MFA from Indiana University, where he was a Yusef Komunyakaa fellow and poetry editor of the *Indiana Review.* He is the author of four collections of poetry: *The Listening* (2004), which won the Cave Canem Prize, *Bouquet of Hungers* (2007), awarded the Hurston/Wright Legacy Award in poetry, *Logorrhea Dementia* (2010), and *Honest Engine* (2015). His poems and non-fiction have appeared in newspapers such as the *Newark Star-Ledger,* and journals such as *Callaloo, Denver Quarterly,* and *Ploughshares,* among others. Former managing editor of *Callaloo,* Dargan is also the founding editor of the magazine *Post no Ills.* He is the Director of Creative Writing at American University and lives in Washington DC.

DANIELLE CADENA DEULEN is the author of three books: *The Riots* (U. of Georgia Press, 2011), which won the AWP Prize in Creative Nonfiction and the GLCA New Writers Award; *Lovely Asunder* (U. of Arkansas Press, 2011), which won the Miller Williams Arkansas Poetry Prize and the Utah Book Award; and *Our Emotions Get Carried Away Beyond Us* (Barrow Street, 2015), which won the Barrow Street Book Contest. She has been the recipient of a U. of Wisconsin Creative Writing Fellowship, three Dorothy Sargent Rosenberg Awards, and an Ohio Arts Council Individual Excellence Award. Her poems and essays have appeared in many journals, including *The Iowa Review, The Kenyon Review, The Utne Reader,* and *The Missouri Review,* as well as several anthologies, including *Best New Poets* and

After Montaigne: Contemporary Essayists Cover the Essays. She is the poetry editor of Acre Books and lives in Salem, Oregon where she teaches for Willamette University.

NATALIE DIAZ was born and raised in the Fort Mojave Indian Village in Needles, California, on the banks of the Colorado River. She is Mojave and an enrolled member of the Gila River Indian Tribe. Her first poetry collection, *When My Brother Was an Aztec,* was published by Copper Canyon Press. She is a Lannan Literary Fellow and a Native Arts Council Foundation Artist Fellow. She was awarded a Bread Loaf Fellowship, the Holmes National Poetry Prize, a Hodder Fellowship, and a PEN/Civitella Ranieri Foundation Residency, as well as being awarded a US Artists Ford Fellowship. Diaz teaches at the Arizona State University MFA program. She splits her time between the east coast and Mohave Valley, Arizona, where she works to revitalize the Mojave language.

DANTE DI STEFANO is the is the author of two poetry collections: *Love Is a Stone Endlessly in Flight* (Brighthorse Books, 2016) and *Ill Angels* (Etruscan Press, forthcoming 2019). He is the poetry editor for *Dialogist* and a correspondent for The Best American Poetry Blog. He lives in Endwell, New York with his wife, Christina, their daughter, Luciana, and their dog, Sunny.

Poet and journalist **CELESTE DOAKS** is the author of *Cornrows and Cornfields* (Wrecking Ball Press, UK, 2015), and most recently the editor of *Not Without Our Laughter* (Mason Jar Press, 2017). *Beltway Poetry Quarterly* listed Cornrows as one of the "Ten Best Books of 2015." Doaks, a Pushcart Prize nominee, is the recipient of a 2017 Rubys Artist Grant. She is the 2017–2018 Visiting Assistant Professor in Creative Writing at the University of Delaware.

MARTÍN ESPADA was born in Brooklyn, New York in 1957. He has published almost twenty books as a poet, editor, essayist and translator. His latest collection of poems from Norton is called *Vivas to Those Who Have Failed* (2016). Other books of poems include *The Trouble Ball* (2011), *The Republic of Poetry* (2006), *Alabanza* (2003), *A Mayan Astronomer in Hell's Kitchen* (2000), *Imagine the Angels of Bread* (1996), *City of Coughing and Dead Radiators* (1993) and *Rebellion is the Circle of a Lover's Hands* (1990). His many honors include the Shelley Memorial Award, the Robert Creeley Award, the National

Hispanic Cultural Center Literary Award, an American Book Award, the PEN/Revson Fellowship and a Guggenheim Fellowship. *The Republic of Poetry* was a finalist for the Pulitzer Prize. The title poem of his collection *Alabanza*, about 9/11, has been widely anthologized and performed. His book of essays, *Zapata's Disciple* (1998), was banned in Tucson as part of the Mexican-American Studies Program outlawed by the state of Arizona, and has been issued in a new edition by Northwestern University Press. A former tenant lawyer in Greater Boston's Latino community, Espada is a professor of English at the University of Massachusetts-Amherst.

JOSHUA JENNIFER ESPINOZA is a trans woman poet living in California. Her work has been featured in *The Offing, Lambda Literary, The Feminist Wire, PEN America, Washington Square Review,* and elsewhere. She is the author of *i'm alive / it hurts / i love it* (boost house 2014) and *There Should Be Flowers* (Civil Coping Mechanisms 2016).

BLAS FALCONER is the author of two poetry collections, *The Foundling Wheel* and *A Question of Gravity and Light*. His awards include an NEA Fellowship, the Maureen Egen Writers Exchange award, and a Tennessee Individual Artist Grant. A poetry editor at the *Los Angeles Review*, he teaches in the MFA program at San Diego State University and in the low-residency MFA at Murray State University. His third full-length poetry collection, *Forgive the Body This Failure* (Four Way Books), is forthcoming in 2018.

KATE FALVEY is the author of *The Language of Little Girls*, a poetry collection (David Robert Books, 2016), and two chapbooks, *What the Sea Washes Up* (Dancing Girl Press) and *Morning Constitutional in Sunhat and Bolero* (Green Fuse Poetic Arts). She is editor-in-chief of the *2 Bridges Review*, which is published through the New York City College of Technology/CUNY, where she teaches. She is also an associate editor of N.Y.U. Langone Medical Center's *Bellevue Literary Review*. Her poetry has appeared in numerous journals and anthologies.

BRIAN FANELLI's most recent book is *Waiting for the Dead to Speak* (NYQ Books), winner of the 2017 Devil's Kitchen Poetry Prize. He is also the author of the collection *All That Remains* (Unbound Content) and the chapbook *Front Man* (Big Table Publishing). His poetry has appeared on *Verse Daily* and "The Writer's Almanac," and it has been published in *The Los Angeles Times, World Literature Today, The Paterson Literary Review, Blue Collar Review, Main Street Rag,* and elsewhere. Brian has an M.F.A. from Wilkes University and a Ph.D. from SUNY Binghamton University. Currently, he teaches at Lackawanna College.

ARIEL FRANCISCO is the author of *All My Heroes Are Broke* (C&R Press, 2017) and *Before Snowfall, After Rain* (Glass Poetry Press, 2016). Born in the Bronx to Dominican and Guatemalan parents, he completed his MFA at Florida International University in Miami. His poems have appeared in *Academy of American Poets, The American Poetry Review, Best New Poets 2016, Gulf Coast, Washington Square,* and elsewhere. He lives in South Florida (for now).

CHRISTINE GELINEAU is a poet and essayist and the author of three full-length collections of poetry: *Crave* (NYQ Books, 2016), *Appetite for the Divine* (Editor's Choice for the McGovern Publication Prize, Ashland Poetry Press, 2010) and *Remorseless Loyalty* (Ashland Poetry Press, 2006), which was awarded the Richard Snyder Memorial Prize, and which was subsequently nominated for the Los Angeles Times Book Award.

MARIA MAZZIOTTI GILLAN is a recipient of the 2014 George Garrett Award for Outstanding Community Service in Literature from AWP, the 2011 Barnes & Noble Writers for Writers Award from Poets & Writers, and the 2008 American Book Award for her book, *All That Lies Between Us* (Guernica Editions). She is the founder/executive director of the Poetry Center at Passaic County Community College in Paterson, NJ, and editor of the *Paterson Literary Review.* She is also director of the Binghamton Center for Writers and the creative writing program, and professor of English at Binghamton University–SUNY. She has published 22 books. Her newest is *Paterson Light and Shadow* (Serving House Books, 2017). Others include *The Girls in the Chartreuse Jackets* (Cat in the Sun Books, 2014); *Ancestors' Song* (Bordighera Press, 2013); *The Silence in an Empty House* (NYQ Books, 2013); *Writing Poetry to Save Your Life: How to Find the Courage to Tell Your Stories* (MiroLand, Guernica Editions, 2013); *The Place I Call Home* (NYQ Books, 2012); and *What We Pass On: Collected Poems 1980-2009* (Guernica Editions, 2010). With her daughter Jennifer, she is co-editor of four anthologies.

JENNIFER GIVHAN is a Mexican-American poet from the Southwestern desert. She is the author of *Landscape with Headless Mama* (2015 Pleiades Editors' Prize) and *Protection Spell* (2016 Miller Williams Series, University of Arkansas Press). Her chapbooks include *Lifeline* (Glass Poetry Press), *The Daughter's Curse* (ELJ Editions), and *Lieserl Contemplates Resurrection* (dancing girl press). Her honors include a National Endowment for the Arts Fellowship in Poetry, a PEN/Rosenthal Emerging Voices Fellowship, The Frost Place Latin@ Scholarship, The 2015 Lascaux Review Poetry Prize, The Pinch Poetry Prize, and her work has appeared or is forthcoming in *Best of the Net, Best New Poets, AGNI, Ploughshares, Poetry, TriQuarterly, Crazyhorse, Blackbird,* and *The Kenyon Review.* She lives with her family in New Mexico.

TONY GLOEGGLER is a life-long resident of New York City. His books include *One Wish Left* (Pavement Saw Press, 2002) and *The Last Lie* (NYQ Books, 2010). *Until The Last Light Leaves* (NYQ Books, 2015) was a finalist in the 2016 Binghamton University Milt Kessler Poetry Book Award. For the past 35 years, he has managed group homes for the mentally challenged in Brooklyn.

RUTH GORING's poetry collections are *Soap Is Political* (Glass Lyre, 2015) and *Yellow Doors* (WordFarm, 2003); she has also published a children's picture book, *Adriana's Angels / Los ángeles de Adriana* (Sparkhouse, 2017). Ruth's poems have appeared in *CALYX, Pilgrimage, RHINO, New Madrid, Crab Orchard Review, Iron Horse Literary Review, Aeolian Harp,* and elsewhere. She edits books at the University of Chicago Press and teaches an editing course at the Graham School for Continuing Liberal and Professional Studies.

SONIA GREENFIELD was born and raised in Peekskill, New York, and her book, *Boy with a Halo at the Farmer's Market,* won the 2014 Codhill Poetry Prize. Her work has appeared in a variety of places, including in *2010 Best American Poetry, Antioch Review, Bellevue Literary Review, Cimarron Review, Cream City Review, Massachusetts Review, Meridian,* and *Rattle.* She lives with her husband and son in Los Angeles, California, where she edits the *Rise Up Review* and co-directs the Southern California Poetry Festival.

GEORGE GUIDA is the author of eight books, including *Pugilistic* (WordTech Editions), his third collection of poems;

The Sleeping Gulf (Bordighera Press), his fourth collection of poems; and *Spectacles of Themselves: Essays in Italian American Literature and Popular Culture* (Bordighera Press), his second collection of critical essays, all published in 2015. His poetry, fiction and essays appear in numerous journals and anthologies. He teaches writing and literature at New York City College of Technology, and is at work on a book about poetry communities around the U. S.

LUKE HANKINS was born in Natchez, Mississippi in 1984 and grew up in Pineville, Louisiana before moving to his current home in Asheville, North Carolina. He attended the Indiana University M.F.A. Program in Creative Writing, where he held the Yusef Komunyakaa Fellowship in Poetry. His first collection of poems, *Weak Devotions*, was published by Wipf & Stock Publishers in 2011. He is also the editor of *Poems of Devotion: An Anthology of Recent Poets*, published by Wipf & Stock in 2012. His chapbook of translations of French poems by Stella Vinitchi Radulescu, *I Was Afraid of Vowels... Their Paleness*, was published by Q Avenue Press in 2011. His latest book, *The Work of Creation: Selected Prose*, was released by Wipf & Stock in 2016. Hankins is the founder and Editor of Orison Books, a non-profit literary press focused on the life of the spirit from a broad and inclusive range of perspectives.

Born in Burbank, California, poet and young adult writer **DAVID HERNANDEZ** earned a BA at California State University-Long Beach. He is the author of several collections of poetry, including *Dear, Sincerely* (2016), *Hoodwinked* (2011), *Always Danger* (2006), and *A House Waiting for Music* (2003), as well as the young adult novels *No More Us for You* (2009) and *Suckerpunch* (2007). Hernandez's honors include a 2011 Literary Fellowship from the National Endowment for the Arts and a grant from the Ludwig Vogelstein Foundation. He has taught at the University of California-Irvine, Antioch University, and California State University-Long Beach. He and his wife, writer Lisa Glatt, live in Long Beach, California.

LUTHER HUGHES is a Seattle native and author of *Touched* (Sibling Rivalry Press, 2018). He is the Founder/Editor-in-Chief of *the Shade Journal* and Associate Poetry Editor for *The Offing*. A Cave Canem fellow and *Windy City Times Chicago: 30 Under 30* Honoree, his work has been published or is forthcoming in *Columbia Poetry*

Review, Vinyl, BOAAT, Tinderbox, The Adroit Journal, and others. Luther is currently an MFA candidate in the Writing Program at Washington University in St. Louis. You can follow him on Twitter @lutherxhughes. He thinks you are beautiful.

KENAN INCE is a mathematician, poet, and musician from Denton, TX, living on occupied Shoshone, Paiute, Goshute and Ute territory (so-called Salt Lake City). Their work has appeared in *Word Riot, Duende,* and *Permafrost,* among others, and has been insulted in the comments section of the Houston real estate blog *Swamplot.*

MARIA MELENDEZ KELSON's poetry collections (*How Long She'll Last in This World* and *Flexible Bones*) have been finalists for the PEN Center USA Literary Award and the International Latino Book Award. Her poetry, feature articles, and fiction appear in *Poetry* magazine, *Ms.* magazine, *Flash Fiction Magazine,* and elsewhere. Her mystery novel-in-progress won the Eleanor Taylor Bland Award for crime fiction writers of color from Sisters in Crime. She has taught writing and literature at Saint Mary's College in Indiana, Utah State University, and Pueblo Community College in southern Colorado, where she is currently a faculty member in English.

RUTH ELLEN KOCHER is the author of seven books of poetry, including *Third Voice* (Tupleo Press, 2016), *Ending in Planes,* winner of the Noemi Poetry Prize, *Goodbye Lyric: The Gigans and Lovely Gun* (The Sheep Meadow Press, 2014) and *domina Un/blued* (Tupelo Press 2013). Her poems have been translated into Persian in the Iranian literary magazine, *She'r,* and have appeared in various anthologies including: *Angles of Ascent: A Norton Anthology of Contemporary African American Poets, Black Nature, From the Fishouse: An Anthology of Poems that Sing, Rhyme, Resound, Syncopate, Alliterate,* and *Just Plain Sound Great, An Anthology for Creative Writers: The Garden of ForkingPath.* She has received grants and fellowships from the National Endowment for the Arts, Yaddo, and Cave Canem. She is currently an Associate Dean for the College of Arts and Sciences at the University of Colorado at Boulder where she teaches Poetry, Poetics, and Literature in the undergraduate and MFA writing programs.

Dana Levin's new book is *Banana Palace* (Copper Canyon Press). She serves as Distinguished Writer in Residence at Maryville University in St. Louis.

Timothy Liu (Liu Ti Mo) was born in 1965 in San Jose, California, to parents from the Chinese mainland. He studied at Brigham Young University, the University of Houston, and the University of Massachusetts at Amherst. He is the author of *Don't Go Back To Sleep* (Saturnalia, October 2014); *Polytheogamy* (Saturnalia, 2009); *Bending the Mind Around the Dream's Blown Fuse* (Talisman House, 2009); *For Dust Thou Art* (Southern Illinois University Press, 2005); *Of Thee I Sing* (University of Georgia Press, 2004), selected by *Publishers Weekly* as a 2004 Book-of-the-Year; *Hard Evidence* (Talisman House, 2001); *Say Goodnight* (Copper Canyon Press, 1998); *Burnt Offerings* (Copper Canyon Press, 1995); and *Vox Angelica* (Alice James Books, 1992), which won the Poetry Society of America's Norma Farber First Book Award.

Former Kansas poet laureate **Denise Low** is the author of twelve books of poetry, including *Casino Bestiary* (Spartan Press), *Mélange Block* (Red Mountain Press) and *Ghost Stories of the New West* (Woodley Memorial Press), a Kansas Notable Book Award and recognized by *The Circle* of Minneapolis as among the best Native American Books of 2010. Low earned her BA, MA, and PhD in English from the University of Kansas, and her MFA from Wichita State University.

George Ella Lyon, the current poet laureate of Kentucky, has published award-winning books for readers of all ages, and her poem, "Where I'm From," has been used as a model by teachers around the world. Originally from the mountains of Kentucky, Lyon works as a freelance writer and teacher based in Lexington, where she lives with her husband, writer and musician Steve Lyon. They have two grown sons.

J. Michael Martinez received the Walt Whitman Award from the Academy of American Poets for his first book, *Heredities*. His latest, *In the Garden of the Bridehouse*, is available from the University of Arizona Press. He is the Poetry Editor of NOEMI Press and his writings are anthologized in Ahsahta Press' *The Arcadia Project: North American Postmodern Pastoral*, Rescue Press' *The New Census: 40 American Poets*, and Counterpath Press' *Angels of the Americlypse: New Latin@ Writing*.

SHANE MCCRAE teaches at Oberlin College and at Spalding University's low-residency MFA in Writing Program. His most recent books are *In the Language of My Captor* (Wesleyan University Press, 2017) and *The Animal Too Big to Kill* (Persea Books, 2015). He has received a Whiting Writer's Award, a fellowship from the NEA, and a Pushcart Prize.

SJOHNNA MCCRAY was born in Cincinnati, Ohio, on March 7, 1972. He studied at Ohio University and earned an MFA from the University of Virginia where he was a Hoyns Fellow. McCray also received an MA in English Education from Teachers College, Columbia University. His poetry collection, *Rapture*, was selected by Tracy K. Smith as the winner of the 2015 Walt Whitman Award from the Academy of American Poets and was published by Graywolf Press in 2016.

ERIKA MEITNER is the author of four books of poems, including *Ideal Cities* (HarperCollins, 2010), which was a 2009 National Poetry series winner, and *Copia* (BOA Editions, 2014). She is currently an associate professor of English at Virginia Tech, where she directs the MFA program in Creative Writing.

RAJIV MOHABIR is the author of *The Cowherd's Son* (Tupelo Press 2017, winner of the 2015 Kundiman Prize) and *The Taxidermist's Cut* (Four Way Books 2016, winner of the Four Way Books Intro to Poetry Prize, Finalist for the 2017 Lambda Literary Award in Gay Poetry). In 2015 he was a winner of the AWP Intro Journals Award as well as a PEN/Heim Translation Fund Grant for his translation of Lalbihari Sharma's *Holi Songs of Demerara*. He received his MFA in Poetry from Queens College, CUNY and his PhD in English from the University of Hawai`i and is currently an Assistant Professor of Poetry at Auburn University.

FAISAL MOHYUDDIN teaches English at Highland Park High School in suburban Chicago, is a past fellow in the U.S. Department of State's Teachers for Global Classrooms program, and has an MFA in creative writing from Columbia College Chicago. His writing has appeared in *Prairie Schooner, Narrative, Painted Bride Quarterly, Catamaran, Chicago Quarterly Review, Poet Lore, RHINO, the minnesota review, Crab Orchard Review, Indivisible: An Anthology of Contemporary South Asian American Poetry*, and elsewhere. He was a finalist in *Narrative*'s Eighth Annual Poetry Contest in 2016 and the recipient of the 2014 Edward Stanley Award from *Prairie Schooner*. Also a visual artist, he lives with his wife and son in Chicago.

A Pushcart Prize winner, Lambda Award finalist and a 2015 New American Poet who has received fellowships to Vermont Studio Center, Rose O'Neill Literary House, Hedgebrook and Cave Canem, **KAMILAH AISHA MOON**'s work has been featured widely, including in *Harvard Review, Poem-A-Day, Prairie Schooner, Best of the Net* and elsewhere. Featured nationally at conferences, festivals and universities including the Library of Congress and Princeton University, she holds an M.F.A. from Sarah Lawrence College and has taught at several institutions, including Rutgers University-Newark and Columbia University. A native of Nashville, TN, she is an Assistant Professor of Poetry and Creative Writing at Agnes Scott College.

ABBY E. MURRAY teaches creative writing at the University of Washington Tacoma, where she offers free poetry workshops to soldiers and military families, serves as editor in chief for *Collateral*, a journal that publishes work focused on the impact of military service, and teaches poetry workshops at Joint Base Lewis-McChord. Her poems can be found in recent or forthcoming issues of *Prairie Schooner, Rattle, Stone Canoe,* and the *Rise Up Review*.

SUSAN NGUYEN hails from Virginia but currently lives in the desert where she is hard at work on her MFA in poetry at Arizona State University. Her previous work has appeared in *PANK, diode, Boxcar Poetry Review,* and others. She is the recipient of two fellowships from the Virginia G. Piper Center for Creative Writing.

MATTHEW OLZMANN is the author of two collections of poems, *Mezzanines*, which was selected for the Kundiman Prize, and *Contradictions in the Design*, both from Alice James Books. His writing has appeared or is forthcoming in *Best American Poetry, Kenyon Review, New England Review, Brevity, Southern Review* and elsewhere. Currently, he teaches at Dartmouth College and in the MFA Program for Writers at Warren Wilson College.

ANNETTE OXINDINE's poems appear or are forthcoming in *Gulf Coast, Southern Indiana Review, Shenandoah, Tinderbox Poetry, Willow Springs, Gargoyle Magazine, The National Poetry Review,* and elsewhere. Originally from Maryland, she lives in Ohio and teaches literature at Wright State University.

GREGORY PARDLO's collection *Digest* (Four Way Books) won the 2015 Pulitzer Prize for Poetry. His other honors include fellowships from the Guggenheim Foundation, the National Endowment for the Arts and the New York Foundation for the Arts; his first collection *Totem* was selected by Brenda Hillman for the APR/Honickman Prize in 2007. He is Poetry Editor of *Virginia Quarterly Review. Air Traffic,* a memoir in essays, is forthcoming from Knopf.

CRAIG SANTOS PEREZ is a native Chamorro from the Pacific Island of Guam. He is the author of three books, most recently from *unincorporated territory [guma']*, which received an American Book Award in 2015. He is an associate professor in the English department at the University of Hawai'i, Mānoa.

XANDRIA PHILLIPS is the author of *Reasons For Smoking,* which won the the 2016 *Seattle Review* chapbook contest judged by Claudia Rankine. She hails from rural Ohio where she was raised on corn, and inherited her grandmother's fear of open water. Xandria received her BA from Oberlin College, and her MFA from Virginia Tech. Xandria is Winter Tangerine's associate poetry editor, and the curator of *Love Letters to Spooks,* a literary space for Black people. She has received fellowships from Cave Canem and Callaloo. Xandria's poetry is present or forthcoming in *Beloit Poetry Journal, West Branch, Nashville Review, Nepantla, Gigantic Sequins, Ninth Letter Online, The Journal,* and elsewhere.

KEVIN PRUFER is the author of six books of poetry and the editor of numerous anthologies, the most recent of which are *Churches* (Four Way Books, 2014), *In a Beautiful Country* (Four Way Books, 2011), *National Anthem* (Four Way Books, 2008), *New European Poets* (Graywolf Press, 2008; w/ Wayne Miller), *Literary Publishing in the 21st Century* (Milkweed Editions, 2016; w/ Wayne Miller &

Travis Kurowski), and *Catherine Breese Davis: on the Life & Work of an American Master* (Unsung Masters, 2015; w/Martha Collins & Martin Rock). His forthcoming book of poems, *How He Loved Them*, will be published by Four Way Books in 2018. His forthcoming edited volume is *Into English: An Anthology of Multiple Translations* (Graywolf, 2017, w/Martha Collins). Prufer is also Editor-at-Large of *Pleiades: A Journal of New Writing*, Co-Curator of the Unsung Masters Series, and Professor in the Creative Writing Program at the University of Houston and the low-residency MFA at Lesley University.

DEAN RADER has published widely in the fields of poetry, American Indian studies, and visual culture. His debut collection of poems, *Works & Days*, won the 2010 T. S. Eliot Poetry Prize, was a finalist for the Bob Bush Memorial Award for a First Book of Poems, and won the 2010 Writer's League of Texas Poetry Prize. His chapbook, *Landscape Portrait Figure Form* (Omnidawn), was named by the *Barnes & Noble Review* as one of the Best Poetry Books of 2013. His newest collection of poems is entitled *Self-Portrait as Wikipedia Entry* (Copper Canyon Press, 2017).

STELLA VINITCHI RADULESCU was born in Romania and left the country permanently in 1983, at the height of the communist regime. She holds a Ph.D. in French Language & Literature and has taught French at Loyola University and Northwestern University. Writing poetry in three languages, she has published numerous books in the United States, France, and Romania. Radulescu's French books have received several awards, including the Grand Prix de Poésie Henri-Noël Villard and the Prix Amélie Murat.

JULIAN RANDALL is a Living Queer Black poet from Chicago. He has received fellowships from Callaloo, BOAAT and the Watering Hole and was the 2015 National College Slam (CUPSI) Best Poet. Julian is the curator of *Winter Tangerine Review's* Lineage of Mirrors. His work has appeared or is forthcoming in publications such as *Washington Square Review, Prairie Schooner* and *The Adroit Journal* and in the anthologies *Portrait in Blues, Nepantla* and *New Poetry from the Midwest*. He is a candidate for his MFA in Poetry at Ole Miss. His first book, *Refuse*, is the winner of the 2017 Cave Canem Poetry prize and will be published by University of Pittsburgh Press in Fall 2018.

CAMILLE RANKINE is the author of *Incorrect Merciful Impulses* (Copper Canyon Press, 2016). She teaches at Brown University and Columbia University and lives in New York City.

ALEXANDRA LYTTON REGALADO's poems and short stories have appeared in *Gulf Coast, Narrative, Notre Dame Review, OCHO, Puerto del Sol* and elsewhere. She is the winner of the St. Lawrence Book Prize and the Coniston Poetry Prize. Her poetry collection, *Matria*, (Black Lawrence Press) is forthcoming in 2017.

ALISON C. ROLLINS was born and raised in St. Louis, Missouri. A Cave Canem Fellow, she is the second prize winner of the 2016 James H. Nash Poetry Contest and her poems have appeared or are forthcoming in *Poetry, River Styx, Vinyl,* and elsewhere. She currently works as the librarian for Nerinx Hall, a high school in Webster Groves, Missouri. In 2016, Rollins was a recipient of the Ruth Lilly and Dorothy Sargent Rosenberg Poetry Fellowship from the Poetry Foundation.

A children's book author and novelist, **LIZ ROSENBERG** attended Bennington College and earned a PhD from SUNY Binghamton. Her collections of poetry include *The Fire Music* (1986), winner of the Agnes Lynch Starret Prize; *Children of Paradise: Poems* (1994); *These Happy Eyes* (2001); *The Lily Poems* (2008), a chapbook; and *Demon Love* (2008). Rosenberg has edited a number of anthologies of poetry for young readers, among them *The Invisible Ladder: An Anthology of Contemporary American Poems for Young Readers* (1996); *Earth-Shattering Poems* (1998), winner of the Claudia Lewis Award for Poetry and New York Public Library Best Book for the Teen Age; *Light-Gathering Poems* (2000), winner of the Lee Bennett Hopkins Poetry Prize; and *I Just Hope It's Lethal: Poems of Madness, Sadness, and Joy* (2005).

NICOLE SANTALUCIA is the author of *Because I Did Not Die* (Bordighera Press). She is a recipient of the Ruby Irene Poetry Chapbook Prize from *Arcadia Magazine* and the Edna St. Vincent Millay Poetry Prize from *The Tishman Review*. Santalucia teaches poetry at Shippensburg University in Pennsylvania and brings poetry workshops into the Cumberland County Prison.

sam sax is the author of *Bury It* (Wesleyan University Press, 2018) and *Madness* (Penguin Books, 2017), winner of the National Poetry Series, selected by Terrance Hayes.

LAUREN MARIE SCHMIDT is the author of three collections of poetry: *Two Black Eyes and a Patch of Hair Missing; The Voodoo Doll Parade*, selected for the Main Street Rag Author's Choice Chapbook Series; and *Psalms of The Dining Room*, a sequence of poems about her volunteer experience at a soup kitchen in Eugene, Oregon. Her work has appeared in journals such as *North American Review, Alaska Quarterly Review, Rattle, Nimrod, Painted Bride Quarterly, PANK, New York Quarterly, Bellevue Literary Review, The Progressive*, and others. Her awards include the So to Speak Poetry Prize, the Neil Postman Prize for Metaphor, The Janet B. McCabe Prize for Poetry, and the *Bellevue Literary Review's* Vilcek Prize for Poetry. Her fourth collection, *Filthy Labors*, is forthcoming from Northwestern University Press in 2017.

RAENA SHIRALI is the author of *GILT* (YesYes Books, 2017). Her honors include a 2016 Pushcart Prize, the 2016 *Cosmonauts Avenue* Poetry Prize, the 2014 *Gulf Coast* Poetry Prize, & a "Discovery" / *Boston Review* Poetry Prize in 2013. Her poems & reviews have appeared in *Blackbird, Ninth Letter, Crazyhorse*, & elsewhere. Most recently, she was the Philip Roth Resident at Bucknell University's Stadler Center for Poetry. She currently lives in Philadelphia & serves as a poetry reader for *Muzzle Magazine*.

SCHEREZADE SIOBAHN is an Indo-Roma social scientist, community catalyst, and hack scribbler. She is the author of a chapbook, *Bone Tongue* (Thought Catalog Books, 2015), a full-length poetry collection, *Father, Husband,* (Salopress UK) and a poetry pamphlet, "to dhikr, i" (Pyramid Editions, forthcoming). She is the creator and curator of The Mira Project—a global dialogue about women's mental health, gendered violence and street harassment.

CLINT SMITH is a doctoral candidate at Harvard University and has received fellowships from Cave Canem, the Callaloo Creative Writing Workshop, and the National Science Foundation. He is a 2014 National Poetry Slam champion and his writing has been published in *The New Yorker, The American Poetry Review, The New Republic, The Guardian, Boston Review, Harvard Educational Review* and elsewhere. He is the author of *Counting Descent* (2016), which won the 2017 Literary Award for Best Poetry Book from the Black Caucus of the American Library Association and was a finalist for an NAACP Image Award. He was born and raised in New Orleans.

MAGGIE SMITH is the author of three books of poetry: *Good Bones* (Tupelo Press, 2017); *The Well Speaks of Its Own Poison* (Tupelo Press, 2015); and *Lamp of the Body* (Red Hen Press, 2005). Smith is also the author of three prizewinning chapbooks. Her poems appear in *Best American Poetry, The Paris Review, Ploughshares, The Gettysburg Review, Guernica, Plume, Virginia Quarterly Review,* and elsewhere. In 2016 her poem "Good Bones" went viral internationally and has been translated into nearly a dozen languages. PRI (Public Radio International) called it "the official poem of 2016."

PATRICIA SMITH is the author of seven books of poetry, including *Incendiary Art* (2017); *Shoulda Been Jimi Savannah* (2012), which won the Lenore Marshall Prize from the Academy of American Poets; *Blood Dazzler* (2008), a chronicle of the human and environmental cost of Hurricane Katrina which was nominated for a National Book Award; and *Teahouse of the Almighty,* a 2005 National Poetry Series selection published by Coffee House Press. Her work has appeared in *Poetry,* the *Paris Review,* the *New York Times, TriQuarterly, Tin House,* The *Washington Post,* and in both *Best American Poetry* and *Best American Essays.*

CHRISTIAN TERESI is the Director of Conferences for the Association of Writers & Writing Programs (AWP). His poems have appeared in several publications including *The American Poetry Review, Crab Orchard Review, The Kenyon Review Online, The Literary Review,* and *Narrative.* He lives in Washington, DC.

LEAH TIEGER is poetry contest editor for *American Literary Review.* Her chapbook, *We and She ...* was published by Finishing Line in 2017, and her poems appear or are forthcoming in *Pleiades, Entropy, Rattle,* and *Menacing Hedge.*

VINCENT TORO's debut collection *STEREO.ISLAND.MOSAIC.* is a winner of Ahsahta Press's Sawtooth Poetry Prize and the Poetry Society of America's Norma Farber First Book Award. He has an MFA in poetry from Rutgers and is a contributing editor for *Kweli Literary Journal.*

LEAH UMANSKY is the author of The Barbarous Century, forthcoming in 2018 from Eyewear Publishing; *Domestic Uncertainties*; and two chapbooks, the dystopian themed *Straight Away the Emptied World* and the *Mad Men* inspired *Don Dreams and I Dream*. She earned her MFA at Sarah Lawrence College and is the curator and host of The COUPLET Reading Series in New York City. Her poems have appeared or are forthcoming in such places as *POETRY, Pleiades, Plume, The Golden Shovel Anthology,* and *The Journal*.

EMILY VOGEL's poetry, reviews, essays, and translations have most recently been published in *Omniverse, The Paterson Literary Review, Lips, City Lit Rag, Luna Luna, Maggy, Lyre Lyre, The Comstock Review, The Broome Review, Tiferet, The San Pedro River Review, 2 Bridges Review,* and *PEN*, among others. She is the author of five chapbooks, and two full-length collections: *The Philosopher's Wife* (Chester River Press, 2011) and *First Words* (NYQ Books, 2015); as well as, a collaborative book of poetry, *West of Home*, with her husband Joe Weil (Blast Press). She teaches writing at SUNY Oneonta and Hartwick College, and lives with her husband, the poet Joe Weil, and their two children, Clare and Gabriel.

JOE WEIL is an assistant professor at Binghamton University. His reviews, essays, poems and short stories have appeared in *Paterson Literary Review, The Literati Quarterly, Rattle, Barnstorm, Blue Collar Review, Lips, The Boston Review, North American Review, Omniverse, New York Times, New York Quarterly, The Louisiana Review, The Saranac Review,* and *Chicago Quarterly Review*, among many others. He has four full-length collections of poetry; his latest collection of poems is *The Great Grandmother Light* published by NYQ Books. In 2013 he was the recipient of the People's Poetry Award by Partisan Press. He has poems forthcoming in *Plume* and *The Comstock Review*. Joe Weil co-founded Monk books with Bianca Stone and Adam Fitzgerald. He has since created Cat in the Sun books with his wife Emily Vogel. Having grown up in Elizabeth, New Jersey, Weil now lives in Binghamton with Emily and two small children, Clare and Gabriel.

JAMEKA WILLIAMS is a graduate of Eastern University in Philadelphia, PA. Her work has been featured in Eastern University's *The Inklings*, Rowan University's *Glassworks Magazine, Prelude Magazine, Gigantic Sequins,* and *Powder Keg Magazine*. She has poetry forthcoming in *Muzzle Magazine* and *Yemassee Journal*. She is enrolled as an MFA candidate at the School of the Art Institute of Chicago. She resides in Chester, PA.

PHILLIP B. WILLIAMS was born in Chicago, Illinois and earned his MFA from Washington University, where he was a Chancellor's Graduate fellow. He is the author of the chapbooks *Bruised Gospels* (Arts in Bloom Inc., 2011), *Burn* (YesYes Books, 2013), and *Thief in the Interior* (Alice James Books, 2016), winner of the Kate Tufts Discovery Award. His poetry has appeared in *Callaloo, Kenyon Review Online, The Southern Review, Painted Bride Quarterly, West Branch, Blackbird* and others. Williams is a Cave Canem graduate and the poetry editor of the online journal *Vinyl Poetry*. He is the recipient of a Whiting Award and teaches at Bennington College.

JANE WONG'S poems can be found in anthologies and journals such as *The Pushcart Prize Anthology XLII, Best American Poetry 2015, The American Poetry Review, Pleiades, Third Coast, jubilat,* and others. Her essays have appeared in *Tin House, CutBank,* and *Black Warrior Review*. A Kundiman fellow, she is the recipient of fellowships from the U.S. Fulbright Program, the Fine Arts Work Center, Squaw Valley, the Bread Loaf Writers' Conference, and Hedgebrook. The author of the book *Overpour* (Action Books, 2016), she holds an M.F.A. from the Iowa Writers' Workshop and a Ph.D. from the University of Washington. Currently, she is an Assistant Professor of Creative Writing at Western Washington University.

JAVIER ZAMORAwas born in El Salvador and migrated to the US when he was nine. He is a 2016-2018 Wallace Stegner Fellow and holds fellowships from CantoMundo, Colgate University, MacDowell, the National Endowment for the Arts, the Poetry Foundation, and Yaddo. *Unaccompanied,* Copper Canyon Press Sept. 2017, is his first collection.